ISBN: 978 1 83632 061 6
Editor: John Carroll
Senior editor, specials: Roger Mortimer
Email: roger.mortimer@keypublishing.com
Cover Design: Steve Donovan
Design: Panda Media and SJmagic DESIGN SERVICES, India
Advertising Sales Manager: Sam Clark
Email: sam.clark@keypublishing.com
Tel: 01780 755131
Advertising Production: Becky Antoniades
Email: Rebecca.antoniades@keypublishing.com

SUBSCRIPTION/MAIL ORDER
Key Publishing Ltd, PO Box 300, Stamford, Lincs, PE9 1NA
Tel: 01780 480404
Subscriptions email: subs@keypublishing.com
Mail Order email: orders@keypublishing.com
Website: www.keypublishing.com/shop

PUBLISHING
Group CEO and Publisher: Adrian Cox

Published by
Key Publishing Ltd, PO Box 100, Stamford, Lincs,
PE9 1XQ
Tel: 01780 755131
Website: www.keypublishing.com

PRINTING
Precision Colour Printing Ltd, Haldane,
Halesfield 1, Telford, Shropshire. TF7 4QQ

DISTRIBUTION
Seymour Distribution Ltd, 2 Poultry Avenue, London,
EC1A 9PU
Enquiries Line: 02074 294000.

We are unable to guarantee the bona fides of any of our advertisers.
Readers are strongly recommended to take their own precautions before
parting with any information or item of value, including, but not limited to
money, manuscripts, photographs, or personal information in response to any
advertisements within this publication.

> *"My grandmother raised five children during the Depression by herself. At 50, she threw her sewing machine into the back of a pickup truck and drove from North Dakota to California. She was a real survivor, so that's my stock. That's how I want my kids to be too."* **Michelle Pfeiffer**

THE UBIQUITOUS PICKUP

American pickup trucks – the most practical of vehicle genres – are absolutely everywhere; rusty old beaters and shiny new ones, two-wheel drive and four-wheel drive models, those from the eras of classic design and the aerodynamic styles of the eighties. So plentiful and hard-worked are they, that it's hard to imagine a country's economy functioning without the pickup.

Somehow though, the pickup is more than just a working tool, it has worked its way deep into American culture beyond just being a means of transport to defining a lifestyle – it's as American as the cowboy and his horse.

This is due in part to the fact that the pickup is the modern day mount of the cowboy and frequently mentioned in songs by the likes of Kip Moore, Willie Nelson, Lee Brice, Rhett Atkins, Brandi Clark and many others. Pickups are invaluable, they haul stuff, tow stuff, can be used for camping and a host of other duties that go towards making them truly indispensable.

This bookazine takes a long hard look at the golden era of the pickup from the 1930s to the 1980s and is liberally illustrated with archive and contemporary photographs of pickups from the major American automakers.

**John Carroll
Editor**

CONTENTS

Introduction

As country singer Joe Diffie notes in one of his songs, *Pickup Man*, there is something out the ordinary about the pickup truck. It might be as American as the Statue of Liberty or the Golden Gate Bridge but that doesn't make it ordinary because the pickup truck as a working tool is inextricably linked to the development of America itself. As surely as the horse and the shovel, so the pickup truck helped shape both a land and a nation. For decades they have been name checked in any number of country songs, starred in all kinds of movies and raced in tough events like the Baja 1000, the annual Mexican off-road race held on the Baja California Peninsula. Somewhere along the road they transformed from being a simple but useful workhorse to fancy toys; ranging from rusty originals to big jacked-up rigs and high-performance hot rods. This rise from the pickup's crude, makeshift origins to the often luxury-item status it is now accorded is quite a tale.

During the first half of the 20th century, during the Great Depression, many Americans were seeking a better life in California. Needing transport and a means of hauling their possessions that could not be fitted in or strapped on a traditional motorcar, they chopped cars down into makeshift trucks with a wooden bed on the back and headed west. In John Steinbeck's seminal novel of this era, *The Grapes of Wrath*, Tom Joad's family loads their possessions into a Hudson sedan converted into a truck. While Ford had been making Model T trucks since 1924, it is perhaps the experience of Okies migrating westwards in search of a better life that ingrained the 'truck' into the American consciousness along with Route 66.

Ford's Model A of 1928 and the Model B that followed established the factory-built pickup along with models from Chevrolet and Dodge, companies that also invested in pickup production in the 1930s and the period of the Great Depression. This began after a major fall in stock prices and led to the Wall Street stock market crash of 24 October 1929. Between 1929 and 1932, worldwide gross domestic product (GDP) fell by an estimated 15%. Some economies started to recover by the mid-1930s but, in many, the negative effects of the crash lasted until the beginning of World War Two. Alongside the tractor, the pickup soon became a useful component of another huge transformation in American society, namely the mechanisation of agriculture.

During World War Two America became, in Franklin D. Roosevelt's words, the 'Arsenal of Democracy'. The phrase came to specifically refer to the industry of the USA as the primary supplier of material for the Allied war effort. It refers to the collective efforts and can-do capitalism of American industry in supporting the Allies. Much of this was concentrated in the established industrial centres of the US, including Philadelphia, Detroit, Cleveland, Los Angeles, Chicago, New York, and Pittsburgh and other cities. The war years spawned two vehicles, that were subsequently influential in the design of post-war pickups, the Willys Jeep and the Dodge WC truck, interestingly both were 4x4.

As well as having shaped America, the history of the pickup can be considered a microcosm of the history of the 20th century that is often referred to as America's century. There were Chevy pickups hauling bootleg liquor through the Prohibition Era, Ford pickups hauling rapidly devaluing goods after the 1929 crash and that beaten up Hudson truck which hauled Tom Joad and his family west to California. There were pickups engaged in the construction of the Hoover and Grand Coulee dams as America worked its way out of the Great Depression. Pickups were carrying Army and Navy personnel about their business on the day that the skies above Pearl Harbor filled with Nakajimas and Mitsubishi Zeroes. Later Dodges and Jeeps splashed ashore on Pacific Islands and Europe to deliver a counterpunch.

RIGHT: **For its stand at the SEMA trade show, Chevrolet built a 1967 C-10 long-bed pickup equipped with the rare large rear-window option. After shortening the frame and cargo box, they applied a coat of Centennial Blue paint and then lowered the suspension. A front disc-brake conversion with genuine Chevrolet parts was installed behind 20-inch forged aluminium wheels that replaced the original steel items. Several classic and modern hot-rodding touches finish off the exterior; smoothed and tucked bumpers and tailgate, brushed aluminium trim and LED lighting inside and out**

Dodges and GMCs hauled the GIs across Europe as part of the Allied armies that destroyed the Nazi tyranny. Trucks would have a place in the changed postwar world too; the guy who delivered parts from the local John Deere dealer brought parts out to the farm in one of the new Fords. Dodges were again painted drab olive as the world heard about the 38th Parallel and in the Deep South trucks bore silent witness to the surfacing racial tensions.

The most popular trucks come from the US 'Big Three' automakers GM, Ford and Chrysler, though some international brands have also entered the market including Toyota and Nissan. Pickup trucks have become

TOP AND ABOVE: **The Ford Model A was the Ford Motor Company's second major success and succeeded the Model T which had been produced for 18 years**

iconic vehicles that are no longer the domain of the farmer or the tradesman. These workhorses have found popularity in a wide range of sectors of the public, ranging from being used as utility vehicles, to being a fashion statement or leisure choice. Where exactly their history will end is unknown but it's surely no accident that there is a thirties truck in a Star Trek episode, The '37s. The makers of the noted sci-fi series and movies, looking ▸▸

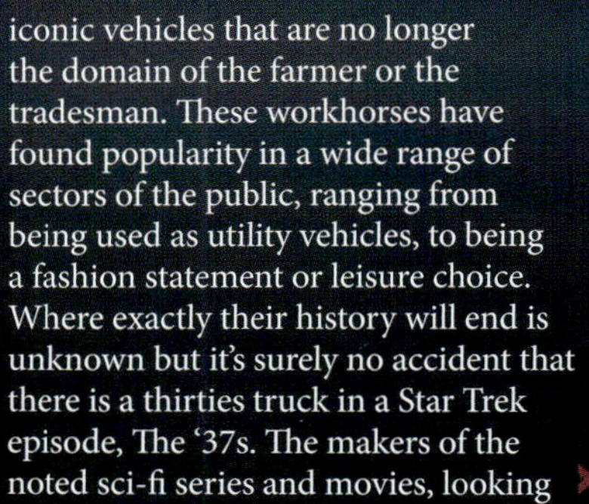

LEFT: **When the Model A was introduced in 1928, it was initially offered only with the open-cab. The closed-cab wasn't offered until August of that year, and exterior colours on all trucks were limited to the buyer's choice of black or green**

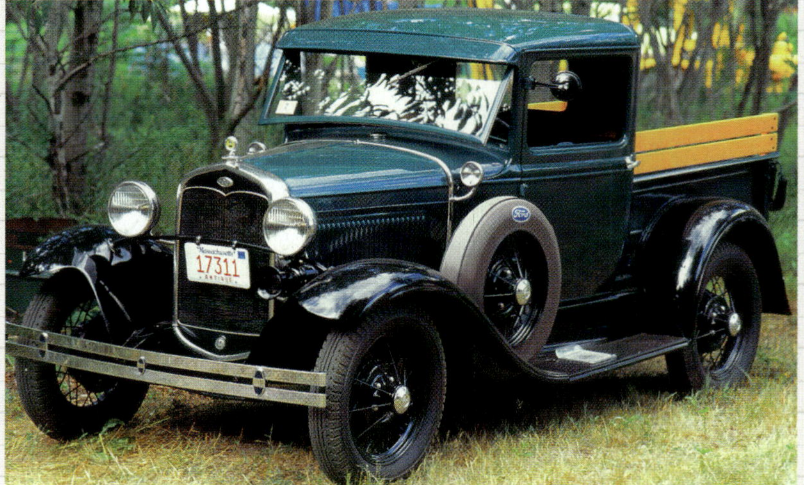

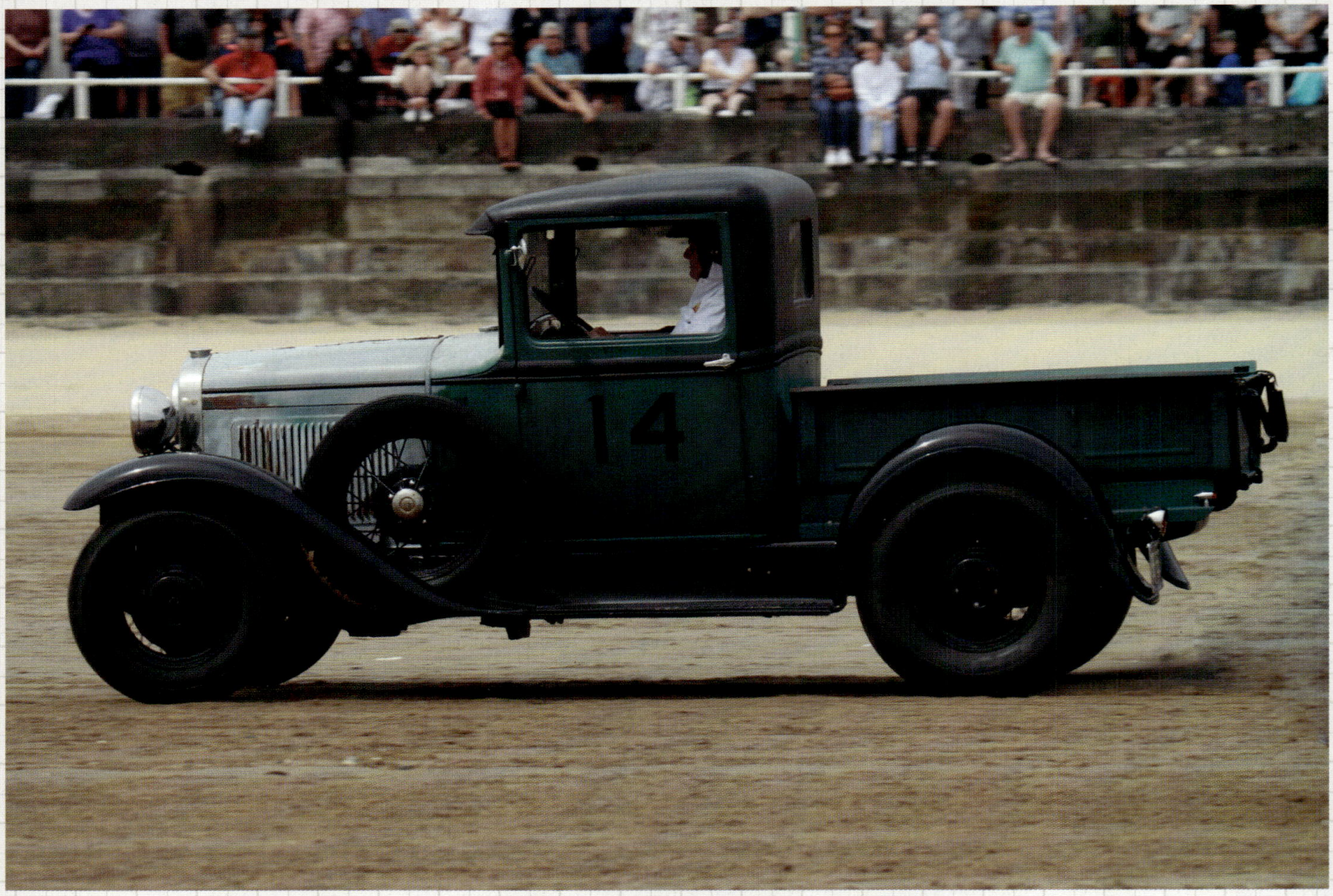

ABOVE AND RIGHT: The Model A pickup's only facelift came in June 1930, when the upright closed-cab was replaced with a lower, rounded and more modern-looking item

for something that encapsulated 20th century America, chose to have a 1936 Ford pickup truck drifting aimlessly through space for the crew of the Starship USS Enterprise to find many generations into the future; something that perhaps give an indication as to just how deeply the pickup truck has worked its way into the American consciousness.

Once the wartime production restrictions of the 1940s were lifted, the competitive scramble to cash in on pent-up demand led to the steady progression of bigger, more powerful trucks detailed in this title. In the late 1940s, Ford's wartime effort towards producing B-24 bombers, Jeeps, tank engines and other military hardware ended and civilian passenger cars and trucks were put back into production, Ford initially produced the same truck and cars from 1941. Following the 1947 model year trucks' introduction, a completely new design was planned for 1948 in the form of the F-1, a new truck for a new era. The vehicle came with a choice of three engine designs, all of which were touted as providing more power and better fuel economy than prior Ford trucks.

Between 1945 and 1980, Dodge developed numerous model series of the Power Wagon, a four-wheel-drive medium-duty truck. For the 1979 model year, the D series was redesigned to have a more rounded appearance. During the 1950s, passenger car styling also started creeping into truck design and by the early 1950s Chevrolet was adding extra windows behind the cab as an option, and also extra body trim options for a deluxe pickup aimed at upscale commercial uses. Internationally renowned industrial designer Raymond Loewy worked with Studebaker on that brand's postwar range of vehicles including pickups. When the all-new Chevy trucks debuted in 1955, they featured wrap-around windshields, hooded headlights and other styling features found on then-current passenger cars.

The scale of postwar pickup production is evidenced by the fact that when, in May 1957, Ford discontinued building trucks at the Highland Park Ford Plant in Highland Park, Michigan, it was able to transfer all light and medium truck production to 10 other plants in the USA. This meant that the second-generation F-Series was produced by Ford at facilities across the

United States. In 1961 Ford offered its styleside pickup with a wide bed and integrated bedsides but there was a problem. The new pickups tied the beds to the body and were termed 'integrated body' as there was no separation between bed and body. When these trucks found use in commercial applications, their doors began springing open suddenly as the weight of the heavy loads was transferred to the body and caused it to flex. Ford reverted to a separate back body for 1962.

The late 1970s were an optimistic time; bell-bottoms were big, disco was on the radio and Happy Days was on TV. At the movies Burt Reynolds was driving that black Trans Am and, in Any Which Way But Loose, Clint Eastwood's character, Philo Beddoe, drove a beaten-up Chevrolet Task Force 3100 truck. Introduced in 1955, it was a truck that blurred the lines between being a working vehicle and a car for everyday driving and this was probably its most famous movie role.

In 1978, more stringent truck emissions standards were on the horizon and fuel prices were rising also, so Dodge made two unusual moves. It offered a Mitsubishi diesel engine in lighter-duty pickups. It was adequate and economical but not enough to offset lack-of-power complaints. For any Ford truck, 1986 marked the end of carburettor engines. It was also the last year for squared-off wheel well openings on the F-Series since rounded wheel wells were adopted with 1987 restyle. The 1987 Ford F-250 marked the start of the eighth product lifecycle for Ford's iconic F-Series of full-size trucks.

Since then, the light-truck market has boomed; trucks have been and remain, the heart and soul that built America, and, as time has passed, the appreciation for the vintage workhorses like Eastwood's Chevy and the Ford F-100 has reached new heights. Classics are both a fun cruiser and a useful household item that are easy to maintain. Pickup trucks can be seen on farms, homesteads, dirt bike tracks, suburban driveways and even parked in executive parking bays in city centres. There is no doubt that the pickup has evolved from being a rural utility vehicle into an American icon. This has led pickup design to include features for various activities from urban to recreational and farming applications. Pickup trucks come in many configurations, depending on their intended purpose; from full-sized light to medium and heavy-duty to luxury trucks, half-ton, three-quarter and one-ton versions as well as regular cab, crew cab, extended cab.

LEFT: The Model A has long been a favourite of hot rodders; Hot Rod Lincoln is a 1955 song by Charlie Ryan that featured a modified Model A and describes a drive north on US Route 99 from San Pedro, Los Angeles, and over the Grapevine Pass that becomes a race

BELOW: A street rod version of the Model A pickup in a style that could be described as resto-rod

The half-ton pickup category refers to the load that the pickup is able to transport in its load bin combined with passenger weight. In other words, it is the truck's maximum load-carrying capacity rather than the weight of the truck itself. Modern half-ton trucks can generally carry more than this load, but the term has become associated with light-duty pickup trucks. »

LEFT: Classic pickup trucks are inextricably part of country music as so many singers and songs reference them

ABOVE: **Dodge, like other US automakers, turned its factories over to war production during World War Two. Dodge's WC (pictured) led to the postwar Power Wagon**

RIGHT: **In the years immediately after World War Two, manufacturers initially restarted production of prewar models to give them time to design new postwar ranges with new styling**

BELOW LEFT AND BELOW RIGHT: **Ford also made trucks for the war effort ranging from 'essential use' pickups and Jeeps, to tank and aeroplane engines**

These trucks are among the most popular for suburban and city residents who are using the truck in place of a car. The interior of a modern light-duty pickup has the features that you would expect to find in a mid-range SUV, and its driving expectations would be for more on-road applications, such as suburban streets and highways, rather than dirt roads and are generally two-wheel-drive models. They make good towing vehicles for small to medium boats and trailers with the Ford F-150 being the most popular light pickup truck in the USA for 2020 by sales alone.

Midsize or medium-duty pickup trucks are ideal for everyday use because they offer a great balance between power and size. These trucks are used by all kinds of people, easily handling everyday tasks and cargo carrying. Such pickups have plenty of room for a family and ample amount of cargo space, but are still manageable around town to drive and park. Historically, a three-quarter-ton truck was a pickup truck that could carry a three-quarter ton - 1500 pounds - as its payload. Because these trucks were considered medium-duty pickup trucks, the name and numerical designation has continued to be used for medium-duty trucks, even though the modern versions of these trucks are capable of carrying more than the 1500-pounds that the name implies.

Heavy-duty or one-ton pickup trucks are in a class all of their own and normally feature large displacement V8 engines. Their suspension makes them capable of carrying heavier or towing loads than the smaller versions. The one-ton pickup truck terminology refers to the modern heavy-duty pickup truck category. Some models in this range feature dual rear wheels, with diesel engines often featuring in these vehicles to better suit commercial loads. The most popular heavy-duty pickups by sales alone in the USA, are the Ford F-Series. The accepted naming convention of a one-ton truck is retained for the historical convention, but versions are usually capable of carrying payloads that exceed the one-ton mark.

The category of 'luxury' pickup trucks is proof enough that these vehicles have made their way into all sectors of the population for a wide range of purposes. Luxury refers to the fit and finish of the interior of the vehicles as well as various add-ons that offer a more comfortable ride and convenience features in the cabin including high-end upholstery, upmarket sound systems, heated seats and advanced electronics.

'Compact Pickup' has different meanings in different locations. »

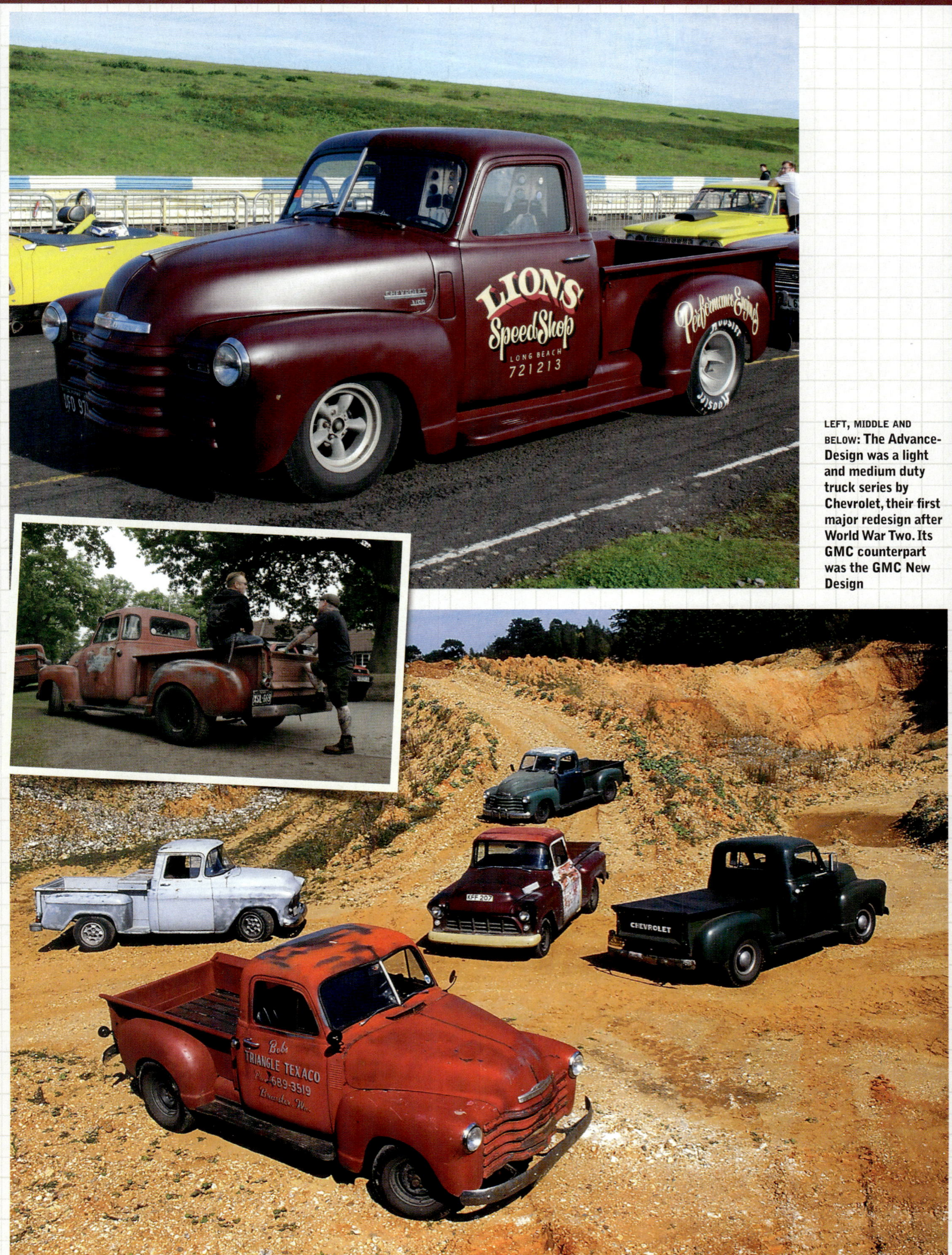

LEFT, MIDDLE AND BELOW: The Advance-Design was a light and medium duty truck series by Chevrolet, their first major redesign after World War Two. Its GMC counterpart was the GMC New Design

ABOVE LEFT: Early Fords remain popular as hot rods and street rods and are not an uncommon sight at drag strips

ABOVE RIGHT: This early Ford pickup has vintage hot rod styling and is powered by the venerable flathead Ford V8

RIGHT: Back in the 1950s, hot rodders in California changed car culture forever with their hot rods and customs. Lyle Fisk was one of those guys, a pinstriper who helped define the traditional custom car style

In some places, it means that the pickup truck has a small load bay and the passenger compartment makes up most of the vehicle. The front-end of these vehicles often looks more like a car than a truck indeed some compact pickups are based on sedan car models. They are typically two-wheel drive, some even being front-wheel drive rather than rear-wheel drive. Compact pickup trucks have lost much of their popularity in recent years, and the fashion has been light-duty pickup trucks.

Because pickup trucks were originally made as workhorses for load transportation rather than people carriers, they had cabs with limited space. Regular cab pickup trucks still conform to this and have a cab that can take two people. If the truck is fitted with a bench seat in the cab, it can

accommodate three people, including the driver. The Ford F-150 trucks from the 1960s to the 1990s all featured a regular cab as the standard model.

A crew cab pickup has four-doors so the vehicle can accommodate a maximum of five adults in the cab; two in the front, including the driver, and three passengers in the back seat. It is termed crew cab because it is intended to carry the crew that you

need for the job that you are going to in your pickup. The load bed of pickup trucks with a crew cab is typically reduced to accommodate the larger cab space of the vehicle. Extended cab pickup trucks are a compromise between regular and crew cabs, they have front seats and rear seats but only two full-sized front doors. Some extended cab models have small courtesy doors that are rear-hinged to provide easier access to the back seat.

The chassis cab pickup comes with a cab, often a regular or extended cab, but no load box. Where the load box would normally sit, the chassis is exposed to make the truck suitable for mounting aftermarket equipment to the chassis in the place of the load box. This could take the shape of a flatbed, a tank bed for transporting liquids, tow truck equipment, or light lifting cranes. These trucks are intended for agriculture and commercial use.

Other types of load bed are stepside, flareside, fenderside, utiline, thriftside and sportside. Really all are different names for essentially the same truck chassis. There are two basic types of truck bed style these days namely »

ABOVE AND RIGHT: The simplicity of 1930s Fords has endeared these old work trucks to another generation of hot rodders

ABOVE AND LEFT:
Chopped and channeled is how hot rods that have had their roof lowered and the body dropped over the chassis rails is described. The result of this is a lower profile rod that will go faster because of reduced wind resistance

FAR LEFT AND LEFT:
Gassers first appeared in the 1950s, and raced until the late 1960s. With a body shell from a vehicle built in the 1930s-1950s (in this case a prewar Willys truck) a big V8, a straight front axle, wide slick tyres to the back and modified suspension they had a distinctive appearance. They are still popular at nostalgia events

INTRODUCTION

ABOVE LEFT: The Ford F-1 is one of the timeless classic pick-ups and as a result is perennially popular in all forms from almost stock or restored to heavily modified. This one is almost stock but runs on chrome wheels

ABOVE RIGHT: The trucks of the late 1950s especially those from Ford, GMC and Chevrolet (pictured) are popular with many

RIGHT: From the late-forties through the fifties and sixties, the big three's trucks evolved year by year; a new design would be launched and then given detail upgrades for a couple of years before being replaced by a completely redesigned model

BELOW: As in any enthusiast car scene some people seek out less well-known models such as this Studebaker seen racing at Race the Waves, a beach event

fleetside and stepside. Fleetsides are slabbed sided with the wheel arches contained within the bed. Chevrolet has used the term fleetside since 1958, while other brands have their own terminology including wideside for GMC while Ford, always being different from its main competitor, uses the term 'styleside.'

A stepside features visible rounded fenders on the outside of the truck bed. This reduces the carrying capacity of the truck bed, but is a popular style. As the name suggests it adds a step to the forward area of the fender where the bed meets the cab. Every manufacturer has its own terms for this style of bed too; Chevy coined the term 'stepside,' which has become a widely accepted term for this type of truck. Ford decided it preferred 'flareside'. It wasn't always this way but currently, stepside trucks are less common as modern truck makers have stopped offering them.

Now in its thirteenth generation, the Ford F-Series is the best-selling vehicle in the U.S. year after year. Over the years, the popularity of the flareside bed has given way to the standard styleside bed. Ford and GM have long been rivals in the pickup truck market. Ford's F-150 competes directly with the Silverado from Chevrolet and the similar Sierra from GMC. Previous versions of these trucks may have carried different names but there have always been comparable models from both manufacturers. Today they include regular cab, extended cab and crew cab models with seating ranging from two to six passengers, as well as different bed lengths being offered. Such modern

trucks aren't bad and pick-ups like the F-150 are unrivalled in strength, reliability, and longevity; still, they are surprisingly cheap.

According to many aficionados, classic trucks are those that are at least 20 years old. Some consider trucks like the GMC Syclone and exotica such as the Italian Lamborghini LM002, as 'collectable trucks' and, although they were designed after 1980, they are still considered classic trucks. Annual

sales of pickups topped two million by 1980 and had surged past 11 million in 2017. This enormous and sustained profitability of its truck line led Ford to limit its future sales of traditional cars in North America. In parallel, because vintage trucks have been steadily gaining popularity with collectors, the cost of such trucks has also risen. However, although the most popular classic pickups are expensive, there are still surprisingly cheap ones available. ★

ABOVE: By the late-sixties, pickups were beginning to resemble the modern pickups that are still in production

ABOVE AND BELOW: **From the 1980s onwards, pickups were marketed as both working tools and recreational vehicles, as these manufacturer photos from Dodge of similar models from the 1990 range illustrate**

ABOVE: **Trucks like the GMC Sierra 400 of the early 1990s were utility pickups with car-like features such as alloy wheels and upmarket sound systems and were intended for daily use instead of a car**

ABOVE: **GMC produced the S-15 that was later renamed the GMC Sonoma. A high-performance version known as the Cyclone, was released in 1991. GMC's LSR (Land Speed Record), a specially prepared 1991 Syclone, was the first truck to break the 200mph barrier. The LSR was clocked at 210.069 mph on the Bonneville Salt Flats**

ABOVE: **A timeless image; 20th century classic pickups are driving into the 21st century future**

DEAN LOWE'S MODEL A ROADSTER PICKUP

Hot rodders like old pickups too and a great example of their enduring popularity is Dean Lowe's 1929 Model A roadster pickup. The story started in February 1960 when, in California, Lowe was given the roadster on his 15th birthday and, with his Dad's help, turned it into a hot rod with junkyard-sourced parts including a '55 265 Chevy engine, before painting it '61 Corvette Roman Red. They raced at El Mirage in 1961 before fitting a 283 Chevy engine. It proved to be an improvement over the previous engine, the car winning its class on Sundays at the Pomona or San Gabriel drag strips. For the 1962 Winternationals drag meet at Auto Club Raceway, Pomona, California, the engine was fitted with fuel injection and seriously tuned and subsequently won its class.

The car survived largely untouched and was eventually taken to England by its new owner, Steve Hill, where it was disassembled and rebuilt. It is now raced in the Vintage Hot Rod Association event at Pendine Sands in Wales. On the beach in 2021 it achieved 121.96mph. This speed meant that it won its class (L8/R) for roadsters with post-1954, eight-cylinder engines. More than half a century later this famous pickup was still setting records.

THE THIRTIES

Depression and Uncertainty

Ford's popular Model T had been replaced by the Model A in 1928 and this meant that Ford soon regained its sales advantage over rival Chevrolet when the Model A car and the Model AA truck started coming off the production lines. The Ford Model AA, half-ton models were available as both Roadster and Closed Cab pickups, with 31 different colours of truck available by 1931. However, the Wall Street Crash of 1929 brought the 'Roaring Twenties' to a sudden

end and ensured that the 1930s would start as a time of considerable economic uncertainty.

The Great Depression started in the United States after the major fall in stock prices, culminating in the Black Tuesday stock market crash of 29 October 1929. The entire automotive industry suffered by the crash, with many automakers almost facing bankruptcy. Between 1929 and 1932 worldwide gross domestic product (GDP) fell an estimated 15%, America's in particular dropping by almost 50% as big business and banking collapsed. The impact to society saw unemployment rise to 25% of the national workforce – an estimated 13 million Americans – by 1932, which meant that people could »

no longer buy consumer goods, such as motor vehicles. In many countries, the effects of The Great Depression lasted until the outbreak of World War II a decade later.

Ford and Chevrolet slugged it out through this period, even as overall industry production totals of automobiles dropped. Chevrolet introduced an in-line six-cylinder engine so Ford retaliated with a V8 in 1932. In the same year total vehicle production was approximated to 1.3 million examples and America elected its first woman senator when Hattie Caraway, a democrat, was elected to represent Arkansas.

New for 1932 would be the Model B Ford, subsequently nicknamed 'The Deuce' which, despite being launched into hard times, became one of the most famous of 1930s' American cars. As a result of their in-line six model, Chevrolet sales soared to the

ABOVE: The '32 and '33 Ford pickup radiator shell is different from the '32 passenger car as it has integral bars rather than a grille insert with a stainless surround and starting crankhole

RIGHT: The roadster pickup in 1932 Model B/B18 and 1933 Model 46/V8-46 forms are the rarest variations made

extent that they were outselling Fords - Henry Ford knew he had to go one better and introduce a V8 model. V8 engines were not new and were already in use in luxury cars such as the Lincolns, built by Ford since it had bought the company from the Lelands in the twenties, but they were not available in mass produced cars and trucks. One of the main reasons for the success of the '32 Ford was that it came with an L-head V8 engine, although a flathead four was an option. The V8 endowed The Deuce with considerable performance and would subsequently endear it to the hot rod fraternity. It has been said by hot rodders that 'The Deuce is one of the few vehicles that looks as good

RIGHT: The 1933 Ford pickup resembled the previous year's model but was based around a 112inch wheelbase chassis unlike the 106inch wheelbase of the 1932 models

with its curved fenders fitted as with them stacked against the garage wall.' The V8-powered truck variant was the Model BB which also appeared in 1932.

The problem in manufacturing a mass-produced, and therefore cheap, V8 was in the difficulty of casting the crankcase block and cylinder banks as one unit. Up until then a V8 had to be cast in three parts, machined and fitted together. Against a background of the Depression times in the auto industry were very hard, even Henry Ford had closed a number of his autoplants and laid off approximately 75,000 workers as his financial resources were over stretched. His pattern makers and foundry men were working day and night to produce the complex V8 blocks, struggling to control 54 separate sand cores. The scrap rate was as high as 100% at times but eventually the casting problem was solved meaning the affordable V8 became a reality. Of this breakthrough, Henry Ford was able to say, "The V8 is the coming car for the majority of American drivers. As always, we have done the pioneer work. It will only be a short time until motor manufacturing practice will follow the trail we have blazed."

The design of the new Ford range progressed under Edsel Ford and designer Joe Galamb while engineer Gene Farkas redesigned the chassis »

This 1933 Ford pickup is fitted with the flathead V8 that was almost new technology when this truck was built. It was sold as a chassis-cab and had a wooden flatbed fitted that was designed for hauling beet

LEFT: The 1934 Model 46 Ford closed cab pick-up was available with four-cylinder and V8 engines. The V8 version was powered by an 85-horsepower engine that displaced 221cid

ABOVE LEFT: The '34 Ford pickup cab has a third extra wide belt line pressed above the two on the '32/33 models to allow the seat back to rest at a slightly less severe angle than the earlier-type cabs. This and the slightly deeper firewall created a slightly roomier cab

ABOVE RIGHT: The commercial '34 Ford half-ton models featured a 112in wheelbase chassis and were available as panel vans, station wagons, chassis-cabs and pickups

MIDDLE: The half-ton DB pick-up of 1934 was Chevrolet's competitor to Ford's trucks. It was introduced in December 1933 and, for the first time since 1918, meant that Chevrolet's trucks had different front sheet-metal to the company's cars

RIGHT: The Chevrolet DB was powered by an in-line, OHV six-cylinder engine of 206.8cid coupled to a three-speed transmission. Standard models had hood sides that featured four vertical louvers

in a way that eliminated the need for splash aprons between the body and running boards (one of the reasons it looks good without fenders). When the 1932 Ford range went on sale, it consisted of 10 car variants and four trucks. The latter vehicles were a sedan delivery, a Murray and Baker-Raulang-bodied station wagon and two pickups. The pickups were a Murray-bodied open-cab and a closed-cab truck. The sedan delivery (with a single side hung door rather than a pair as in a panel van), the station wagon woody, and open-cab pickup were built in small numbers, production totalling 2371 for all three, but 14,259 of the closed-cab pickups rolled off the Detroit line. Most of them were four-cylinder powered because the V8 was not available for them until late in the model year. The Murray-bodied open-cab pickup was assembled from parts of other Fords including Model A leftovers but the closed-cab pickup featured a new all-steel body that shared styling and parts with the cars. Sales of the 1932 models were slow mainly as a result of the depression, with Ford recording a loss of $75 million. However, the new engine can be attributed with the re-establishment of Ford's position as the leading automaker.

The depths of the depression were plumbed in 1933 as thousands of dust bowl farmers from Oklahoma and the surrounding regions drove west in search of a better life. Ford's range for the 1933-34 sales season included sedan deliveries that followed the

lines of the redesigned car range while the roadster and closed-cab pickup models remained more like the 1932 range in appearance.

Ford managed to stay ahead of Chevrolet in the numbers of trucks sold, although things also progressed rapidly for Chevrolet through the 1930s; hydraulic shock absorbers, vacuum windscreen wipers, electric fuel gauges and external rear view mirrors had all become standard equipment in 1930 for example. Chevrolet acquired a specialist truck body maker - Martin Parry Corporation - in the same year that led to the company's offering a range of half-ton pickups, panel vans and canopy express trucks as factory

LEFT: For 1935 Chevrolet's half-ton pickups were designated EB light delivery models and nine versions were offered on a 112inch chassis with an-line six-cylinder engine of 26.8cid

BELOW: In the early thirties, Dodge introduced designations for its trucks that used advancing letters to correspond to model years and a C suffix to designate truck. Pictured is a 1934 KC half-ton pickup

models. The acquisition of Martin Parry would boost Chevrolet's sales in the light truck market far beyond the 32.7% sales penetration they had already achieved by this time. Through the 1930s Chevrolet offered a range of colours, a synchromesh transmission and pushed their trucks hard through fleet sales. All these things contributed to the company's market share climbing from that achieved in 1930 to 50% in 1933, the same year as they produced their millionth truck. As the 1930s moved on Chevrolet trucks became more streamlined and styled in the manner of their passenger cars, certain models shared the same front-end sheet-metal. The range included larger capacity trucks including three-quarter and one-ton models. Progress continued and in 1934 Chevrolet »

LEFT: Ford's range of trucks was restyled for 1935 to incorporate a new and narrower grille that gave a more streamlined appearance. The pictured V8-powered closed-cab was the Model 50 830 while other variants such as panel vans and chassis-cabs were 810, 820 and 840

trucks came equipped with hydraulic brakes - referred to in the slang of the time as 'juice-binders' - and the cabs were built with one-piece steel roofs. This year saw the overall total number of trucks produced increase slightly over 1933 as America began to slowly recover from the financial hardships.

Introduced in 1933 had been a range of trucks completely designed by Chrysler. The new range featured an in-line, six-cylinder engine, something that would endure until the 1960s, and distinctly car-like styling of the time. During the thirties IHC used alphabetical designations for its trucks, the A series was manufactured between 1930 and 1932, the C series from 1933 to 1934 and so on. There was no Series B, presumably because Ford was already using a similar designation at that time. Of these trucks the AW-1, for example, was a conventional three-quarter-ton truck powered by a four-cylinder engine and available in either

ABOVE: Also offered by Ford for 1935 were larger capacity versions of the pickup. These included Model 51 truck in one and 1.5ton pickups and chassis cabs with 131.5inch and 157inch wheelbases such as this fuel tanker

RIGHT: For the 1936 model year the radiator grille was slightly revised and the half-ton pickup marketed as the Model 67 and 68 830 in V8 and four-cylinder forms respectively

chassis, panel, pickup, canopy truck, screen-side or sedan delivery configurations. The later Model C series for 1935 included the C-1, C-10, C-20 and M-3. The C-1 models were the half-ton line in both 113- and 125inch wheelbases. The C-10 models were three-quarter-ton trucks on a 133inch wheelbase. The C-20 models were larger trucks based on a 157inch wheelbase and a maximum capacity of around 1.5 tons. The M-3 was a 133inch wheelbase one-ton truck. It was during the 1930s that GMC really started mass production of light trucks. Its early 1930s models had styling comparable with Fords of the day; cabs had vertical windshields, while hoods were long with louvred sides. The range for 1932 included the T-11 half-ton, T-15 three quarter-ton, T-15AA and T-17A one-ton models.

In 1935 the UAW (United Auto Workers) Union was formed and affiliated to the Congress of Industrial Organisations (CIO). The Chevy truck range for this year included »

LEFT: Production of the 1936 models continued into 1937 until the restyled 1937 models were announced

BELOW: Dodge announced an all-new line of trucks and commercial cars for 1936 including the LC half-ton panel van. They featured new styling that included rounded contours and curved lines

LEFT: A drag race-prepared Dodge pickup. Dodge introduced the LC trucks in November 1935 and produced 109,392 trucks of all types (including larger ones) for calendar-year 1936. Of these 8,599 were manufactured in the company's Los Angeles plant while 2,764 were built in Canada

ABOVE LEFT: For the half-ton trucks in the LC commercial line, Dodge used a single 116inch wheelbase although the three-quarter ton LE trucks were available in three wheelbases. This carried through into the MC/MD trucks for 1937

ABOVE RIGHT: For 1937 Ford's sedan deliveries and coupe pickups were considerably redesigned but its conventional pickup models much less so. The revised grille featured horizontal bars and a two-piece windshield was fitted. This, 830 pickup was available as the Model 73 with a 60hp V8 and the Model 77 with a 85hp V8. Both were flatheads and displaced 136 and 221cid respectively

RIGHT: All the early Fords are popular as hot rods and this 1937 truck is no exception with its patinated paintwork and faux vintage signwriting

Model EC and EA sedan delivery, EB suburban and various EB pickups. For 1936 Chevrolet would add a coupe delivery to the range, based on the FC series of passenger cars. A redesigned Ford range appeared in 1935, the year that Fords were the best-selling cars and trucks in the USA. The restyle incorporated a new narrower grille, a longer hood and more rounded fenders. This design was only slightly revised for 1936 with minor changes to the wheels and radiator grille shell. Appearing in 1937 was Fords unusual truck, based on a standard coupe car with a pickup body. Its introduction was intended to compete with Chevrolet's coupe delivery of the previous year, however, coupe pickups were poor sellers for both companies and Ford discontinued its model at the end of that same model year although Chevrolet persevered with their version until the outbreak of World War Two. Plymouth commercial vehicles were offered between 1935 and 1942 alongside Dodge trucks, as both companies were part of the Chrysler group. Plymouth was the low-cost brand and the same strategy as with their cars was employed with pickup sales where dealers with joint Chrysler-Dodge franchises were offered an opportunity to increase their sales.

Pivotal Year

In engineering terms 1936 saw numerous achievements; construction of the Hoover Dam was completed in the United States, the British liner RMS Queen Mary made her maiden voyage across the Atlantic and Indian Motorcycles' main rival, Harley-Davidson, introduced its first overhead valve V-twin motorcycle with Art Deco influenced design features. On the world's stage, the clouds of uncertainty and war were gathering in Europe and North Africa; the Spanish Civil War started, the Italians annexed Ethiopia to create Italian East Africa and King Edward VIII abdicated from the British throne. The 1936 Summer Olympics took place in Nazi Germany, where African-American athlete Jesse Owens won four Gold Medals. The GMC truck range was redesigned for 1936 and again for 1937, the T-14 of 1937 was a half-ton truck powered by a 230 cubic inch displacement in-line six-cylinder engine. The front end featured a vertical grille with bullet shaped headlights positioned between the fenders and the sides of the hood while the remainder of the truck was of a basic configuration that would endure for several years. The T-16L was a three-quarter ton version of the same model and the FL-16 was a walk-in delivery van version. In 1937 almost 35,000 GMC trucks were registered and the company offered a similar range for 1938 although the headlights were then mounted on the sides of the hood.

The Model 77 pickup was the half-ton Ford for 1937 and was powered by the 136cid version of the flathead V8 although a larger capacity version was optional hence the V8 badges on the hood sides

1937 was both the year that Studebaker introduced a truck and San Francisco's Golden Gate Bridge was opened to traffic. Studebaker sales were good and the company would remain in the pickup business until the closure of its Indiana plant in 1963. Their 1937 model was the coupe express which sourced most of its front sheet-metal from the, surprisingly named, Studebaker 5A Dictator car of the time. This truck was based around a 116inch wheelbase and power came from an in-line six-cylinder L-head engine of 217.8 cubic inch displacement. For 1938 the pickup was also based on the concurrently produced car and again featured the same front end »

ABOVE: For 1937 GMC light duty trucks were given a redesigned front end including the grille that now featured three groups of horizontal bars and repositioned headlamps. In half-ton form it was known as the T-14A and in three-quarter-ton form it was the T-16L

RIGHT AND BELOW: Dodge's 1937 MC models were slightly redesigned into the RC models like this half-ton pickup for 1938. The grille became more like Dodge cars of the time but was not identical and a more comprehensive redesign would follow for 1939

sheet-metal. Specialist machines were also offered and included large capacity furniture vans, fire trucks and similar. Again, for 1939 the pickup was to share its front end with Studebaker's car line so the truck was restyled again.

IHC had expanded its truck line in 1936 to include seven basic truck models within its range. They all had styling similar to the 1935 models. This included a tall V-shaped grille,

long hood with louvred sides, a tall cab and curved fenders that ran back to join the running boards. The smaller displacement trucks used Waukesha four-cylinder engines while the larger models used an in-line six. A redesigned line of IHC trucks - the D-series - debuted in the spring of 1937. The appearance of the new models was considerably different as a result of redesigned grilles, two-

LEFT AND BELOW: A 1938 Chevrolet Model HD three-quarter ton pickup that has been the property of one family for half a century

piece windshields and a fat-fendered appearance. The all-steel cab styling was referred to as 'turret-top styling' by its maker. This new range helped IHC increase its lead over Dodge and retain the third position in sales in the USA with 30.22% of the total truck market. The figure would drop considerably to only 10.24% for 1938 but surprisingly still leave IHC in third position. The IHC trucks continued almost unchanged for 1939 and IHC sales improved slightly to give the company 11.38% of the total US market. »

LEFT: International Harvester introduced a new line of trucks in the spring of 1937 and subsequently made minimal changes across its 1937-39 models that were offered as the D-2, D-5 and D-15 with wheelbase soft 113, 125 and 130inch respectively. The D-2 and D-5 were half-ton models while the D-15 was rated as a three-quarter ton truck

ABOVE: By 1939, a one-ton version that required more substantial wheels had been added to the range that proved popular for specialist applications such as this fuel tanker

RIGHT: Dodge's redesigned trucks for 1939 were promoted to customers in brochures such as this that draws attention to the vehicle's 116inch wheelbase

The first commercials from Plymouth were 'commercial cars' - passenger cars produced with a sedan delivery body. Production was numerically small but considered sufficiently worthwhile by the company for them to increase the range from 1938 onwards. For 1939 the range included the PT81 pickup powered by an in-line six-cylinder engine driving through a three-speed transmission. Slightly more than 6000 of these trucks were produced. By 1940 the company was offering the PT105 pickup truck that closely resembled the Dodge trucks of the time. It was powered by an in-line six-cylinder engine of 201.3 cubic inch displacement that produced 79 bhp@3000rpm. The truck was based on a 116inch wheelbase chassis. The slightly upgraded models for 1941 became the PT125 series and these pre-war models were the last trucks from Plymouth for 33 years.

Things changed significantly again at Ford in 1938 when its trucks came assembled with a chassis that conformed to the specifications of the American Society of Automotive Engineers' (ASAE) recommendations which included better brakes and larger diameter wheels. For 1938 Ford had also offered a range of one-ton trucks to complement its existing half-ton models. Things continued to improve and for 1939 Ford trucks were equipped with 'juice binders'. The range had also been expanded to make it even more comprehensive with the addition of three-quarter-ton models. These trucks featured a rounded radiator grille shell, more rounded fenders and steel wheels instead of the spoked wire items used until now.

GMC was aware of the changing trends and its range was redesigned for 1939. Their windshields became two-piece and although the grille remained vertical it was redesigned to incorporate heavier looking horizontal inserts. The company offered four six-cylinder-powered, half-ton models on a 113.5inch wheelbase and three similarly engined models with a 123.75inch wheelbase. The half-tonners were designated the Series AC-100 and AC-102 trucks, while the greater payload models were the AC-150, AC-250 and ACL-300. In the various capacities there were chassis, chassis-cab, pickup and panel van models and in the larger capacity trucks there were also platform, stake-bed and express models. This range was developed for the 1940 model year and walk-in delivery vans of a forward control design (where the driver sits over or forward of the front axle) were added to the range.

In 1939 Ford of Canada was conscripted into the war effort to build a range of military vehicles as in Europe, Hitler's German armies had invaded Poland on 1 September. Canada joined the war in support »

ABOVE: A patinated example of the 1939 Dodge at a beach race event. To build its new models, Dodge opened the world's largest pickup truck factory in Warren, Michigan, where it still builds pickups

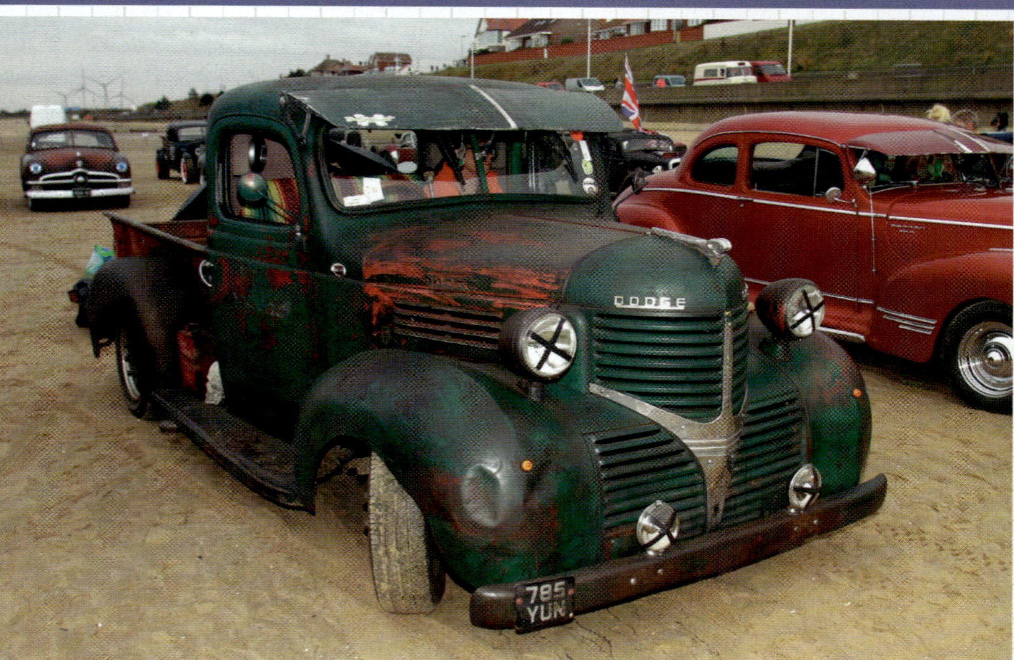

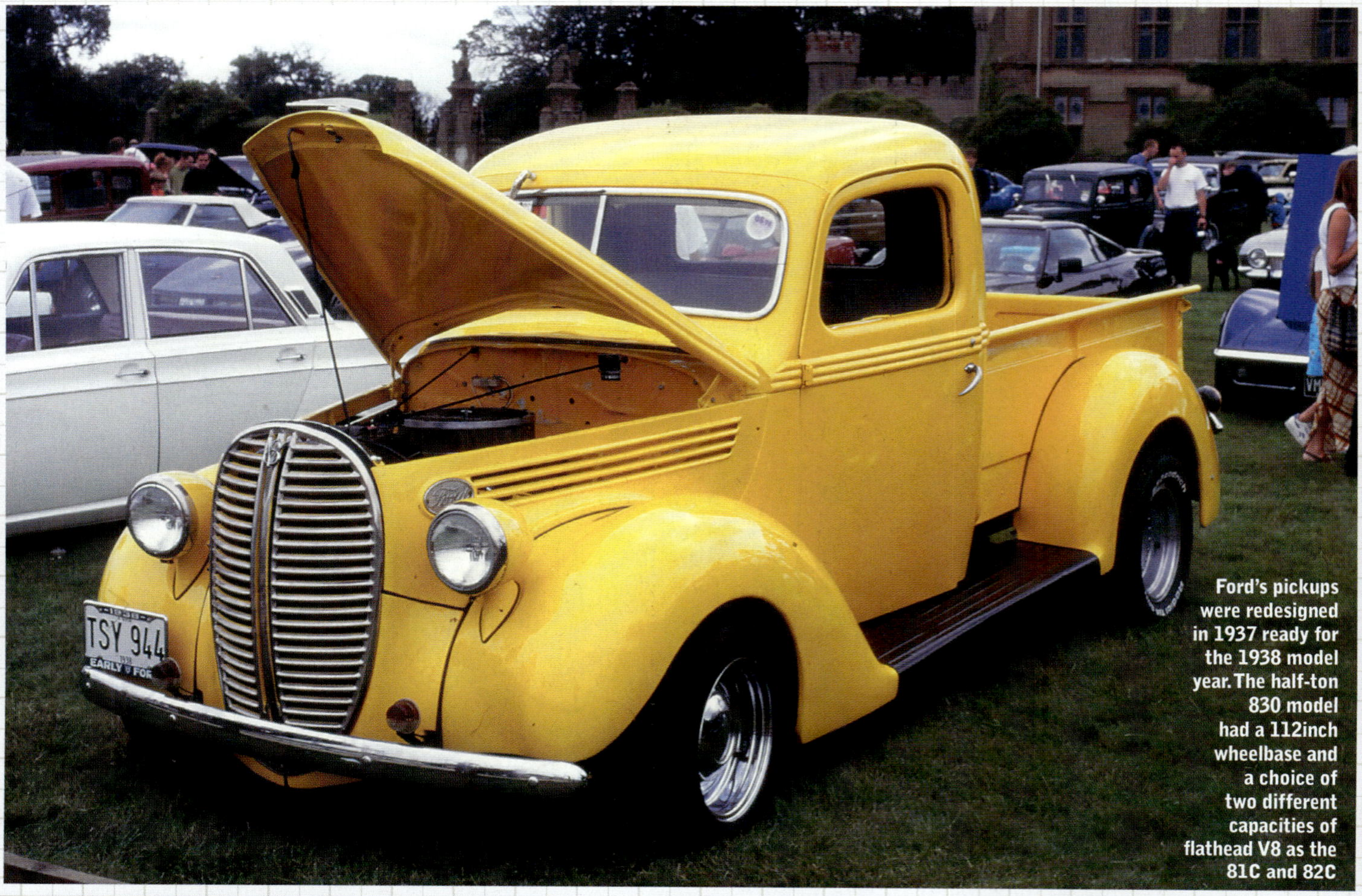

Ford's pickups were redesigned in 1937 ready for the 1938 model year. The half-ton 830 model had a 112inch wheelbase and a choice of two different capacities of flathead V8 as the 81C and 82C

ABOVE AND RIGHT: Like its predecessors, the 81C/82C half-ton Ford pickup was available with a choice of displacement flathead V8 engines and a 112inch wheelbase

ABOVE AND LEFT: The 1938 Ford pickup gained a new egg-shaped radiator grille that comprised numerous horizontal bars divided by a vertical trim piece. These were completed by horizontal hood-side louvers

of Great Britain, who had declared war on Germany on 3 September 1939, after the Nazis refused to withdraw their troops from Poland. With an eye to world affairs, President Roosevelt declared a 'limited emergency' within a week of the beginning of war in Europe and permitted further recruiting to both the US Army and The National Guard. The process had actually started earlier that summer when the strength of the army had been increased from 175,000 to 210,000. General Marshall, recently appointed Chief of Staff, established several tactical corps HQs with enough troops to create a fully functioning field army. The uncertainty ahead and the coming war would irrevocably change the entire world especially the methods of industrial mass production and automobile design. ★

THE FORTIES
War and Peace

The Ford Motor Company unionised on 21 June 1940, but this development in industrial relations was generally overshadowed by world events. America watched as World War II broke out in Europe, and it was apparent that the US Army had fallen behind in their doctrine; the German Army had modernised while the US Army had not.

While mechanisation of the US Army had commenced in 1936 it had been a slow process due to a lack of funds. While war raged in Europe, America initially remained an uneasy

The 1940 Dodge had bodywork that ran from 1939-1947. They featured streamlined styling, a ventilating windshield and numerous mechanical upgrades

bystander, but in 1940 an amount of expenditure was permitted to enable the US Army to procure much needed motor transport. The reason for this was partially that the reorganisation of the army intended that non-divisional cavalry in the form of cavalry recce squadrons would ride 'point' ahead of the new divisions. Each squadron would consist of three recce troops and nine recce platoons that would be transported in a defined number of White Scout cars, Dodge Command Cars and motorcycles.

General Marshall reorganised the basic infantry divisions into five three-regiment 'triangular' divisions and aimed to make them more manoeuvrable and flexible. In May 1940 the first corps manoeuvres held since 1918 took place and grew in size through the summer of that year. These were followed by the huge Louisiana Manoeuvres of September 1941, a series of four exercises that took place over two separate venues – the Louisiana-Texas border and the Carolinas – with each spanning vast, scarcely populated areas of dense forests, uncharted swamps, and river crossings where around 472,000 troops bivouacked »

ABOVE: These 1940 models were the first time since 1932 that the truck models shared the car's styling

RIGHT: The curved body panels, distinctive styling and flathead V8 engines have endeared the '40 Ford to hot rodders

RIGHT: Chevrolet restyled its trucks' front ends and carried this styling forward for 1940 but relocated the side lights onto fenders

for the largest simulated battle in US history over the course of five days. These manoeuvres were a logistical achievement and were a place to test and train for emerging operational concepts. The early manoeuvres featured a clash between the US Army's past and its future. Horse troopers were pitted against armoured units but it soon became evident that mechanisation would replace the horse as motorcycles, the newly developed light 4x4s, Bantam BRC, Willys MA and Ford GP (predecessors of the Willys MB Jeep), and larger trucks from established automakers were deployed alongside tanks during the exercises.

On the civilian market, new for 1940, was the 'Forty Ford' range of vehicles that are generally acknowledged as being some of Ford's most distinctive trucks ever. The new trucks featured styling similar to the cars for that year with a graceful hood that comes forward to finish almost in a point. The rear sheet-metal varied depending on the type of vehicle in a range that included a panel van, pickup and stakebed truck. There were half, three-quarter and one-ton variants that had 112, 122 and 122inch wheelbases respectively. The coupe pickup reappeared for 1941 and the radiator grille and hood designs varied between the trucks with differing payloads. Marmon-Herrington offered a 4x4 conversion to the three-quarter ton Model 11D Pickup. Willys Overland was producing similarly styled trucks with hoods that finished in a point at

the same time. These had progressed
from a flat grille with the introduction
of the Model 77 in 1937 that became
the Model 38 in 1939 and the Model
441 in 1940. In the latter years the
company produced a total of 32,930
cars, trucks and MA Jeeps.

  IHC introduced its Model K truck
during the autumn of 1940 for the
1941 model year. The styling was
modern with integral fenders that
incorporated headlights and a smaller
vertical grille and a rounded hood.
The new series was powered by the
green diamond in-line six-cylinder
engine. With only minor changes
this design would take IHC up to
the outbreak of war. A new line of
Studebaker pickups was introduced »

RIGHT: In June 1940, with World War Two on the horizon, the US Army solicited bids from automakers for a quarter-ton 4x4 truck tailored to army specifications. Willys-Overland delivered its prototype 'Quad' in November 1940

BELOW: Also preparing for conflict was Dodge that built the 4x4 WC series for the US Army. Pictured is a 1941 pattern WC4 on a muddy stretch of the Alaska Highway near Fort St John in British Columbia during 1942

for the 1941 model year, tagged the M series. They used a common cab and front end, both of which were unique to the truck line. The truck was built with economic priorities in mind so that the running boards were interchangeable from side to side to minimise production costs and the front and rear fenders were interchangeable on a given side. An I-beam front suspension system was used on the 113inch wheelbase truck, that was powered by an in-line six-cylinder engine. The company sold more than 8000 in the first year of production.

Pearl Harbor

The Japanese air strikes against Pearl Harbor in Hawaii, Guam and the Philippines on 7 December 1941, pushed the American nation into World War Two, via an Act of Congress the day immediately after the airstrike. Within days the United States Marine Corps were fighting a desperate action to hold Wake Island. Wake Island is a tiny Pacific atoll that up to that point had been used almost exclusively by Pan American Airways to refuel huge flying boats on around the globe services. The US Marines' determined stand for 16 days against overwhelming odds became the lead story in numerous editions of US newspapers. It was also the first sign, so soon after the disaster at Pearl Harbor, that although the road to victory would be long and massively costly, America, the most powerful industrial nation on earth, would ultimately win.

In the final years before US involvement in World War Two, the GMC trucks were redesigned again and most of them redesignated as CC Series trucks. The redesign moved the headlights out onto the fenders, saw a new horizontal barred grille fitted and incorporated the sidelights into the

tops of the headlight cowls. The styling remained the same for 1942 models until production was suspended for the duration of the conflict. The outbreak of World War Two saw White moved to Scout Car production and Dodge continuing to produce the WC range of 4x4, half-ton vehicles that had been introduced in 1936. Of these, open-cab pickups/weapons carriers were the most numerous of the WC series, although closed-cab pickups were also manufactured. In 1942, these were superseded by a range of three-quarter-ton models. These vehicles included a three-quarter-ton 4x4 chassis that served as the basis for WC51 weapons carriers, WC54 »

LEFT: Willys refined its Quad into the MA by 1941. It featured a gearshift on the steering column, low-side body cut-outs and two circular instrument clusters on the dashboard. This would be further refined into the Willys MB for mass production and laid the foundations for post-war 4x4 trucks

RIGHT: American personnel carrying out maintenance on a 1941 US Army G-506 truck, the Chevrolet G7100 1.5ton, 4x4 truck of which more than 150,000 were made

BELOW LEFT AND BELOW RIGHT: Civilian vehicle production did not stop until after the attack on Pearl Harbor in December 1941 so sedans for that year got a new body, but pickups retained the 1940 shape. However, the 1941 pickup gained a wider chrome garnish running down the nose of the hood

ambulances and WC56 command cars. Dodge became the largest producer of this type and while the ambulances were frequently referred to as 'meat wagons' the weapons carriers were often known as 'Beeps', an acronym for 'big Jeeps'.

The WC series trucks were a common sight in both the European and Pacific theatres of operations during World War Two and only superseded in 1950 by the Dodge M37. This military vehicle was such a success that post-war, a version of it known as the Power Wagon, would be introduced for the civilian market. Other truck makers also assisted in the war effort. During the conflict IHC manufactured a range of machinery including a 4x4 half-ton pickup and half-track vehicles for the allied armies. The company produced more than 13,000 International M-5 half-tracks at its Springfield plant. The company also made an amount of 'essential use' pickups for civilians who required transport in order to assist the war effort. Willys Overland received a truck manufacturing stop order from the War Production Board on 4 March 1942, and completely turned its production over to the quarter ton 4x4 Jeep MB.

Ford's civilian pickup trucks were redesigned again for 1942, but then the company's focus turned to winning the war. The V8 Ford Model GC was a military specification 4x4 pickup truck. Another of Ford's significant contributions to the allied cause was to turn some of its production capability over to building Willys MB Jeeps because Willys did not have the vast production capacity required. The Ford assembled Jeeps were designated Ford GPW with the company also producing an amphibious »

Ford's 1940/41 three-quarter, one and 1.5ton pickups were built on a heavier, longer chassis with completely different front sheet-metal and 1939 style fenders with the headlights on top. They were available in pickup, panel, platform and stake-bed versions with a choice of three engines

LEFT: The 1942 Ford pickup was restyled with a slightly protruding felt front panel that incorporated the headlamps and the so-called 'waterfall' grille comprising vertical bars

BELOW LEFT AND BELOE RIGHT: For the 1941 model year Chevrolet redesigned the front sheet-metal of its A series trucks to incorporate the headlamps in the fenders. This front-end treatment would survive World War Two and remain in use until 1946

ABOVE: Dodge's WC pre-war front-end styling of 1939 would also be interrupted by war, so stayed in use until 1947

RIGHT AND BELOW: The second generation of the 4×4 WC Dodge trucks were built from 1942, when the payload was uprated, and the trucks became the shorter G-502, WC series 3/4-ton, 4×4 Truck (Dodge). The WC52 pictured differed from the WC51 by having a front-mounted winch

variant of the same vehicle which was designated GPA. When the war ended Willys had built 358,489 MB Jeeps and Ford had built 277,896 of the GPW. The Willys MB Jeep and the Ford GPW versions undoubtedly laid the foundations for the post-war mass-produced 4x4 pickup.

At Chevrolet civilian truck production ended in January 1942, although the company later obtained permission to build a number of trucks to 1942 specifications for high priority civilian use. Large-scale civilian truck production did not start on the Chevrolet lines again until 1944. The numerous trucks produced for the allied cause during World War Two meant that they were the main supplier of 1.5-ton 4x4 trucks to the US Army. These trucks were of a standardised design powered by a six-cylinder in-line petrol engine, driving through a four-speed transmission and two-speed transfer case. The chassis was of a steel ladder type with leaf sprung suspension. A steel closed-cab of a conventional design and a cargo rear body and canvas tilt completed the NJ-G-7107 as it was tagged. All Chevrolet plants participated in the production effort with the exception of Saginaw, that exclusively made spares for the civilian Chevrolets already on the road.

Studebaker was another of the manufacturers permitted to produce a limited supply of trucks for essential civilian use towards the end of the war. Chrysler made Sherman tanks and Pontiac made anti-aircraft guns.

Peacetime Production

The war seriously interrupted things for the truck manufacturers as it had every other walk of life. From most of the major manufacturers 1946-48 model year trucks were essentially nothing more than slightly improved pre-war machines. For their immediate post-war trucks, Ford kept the design features of the last pre-war models »

ABOVE: **A restored 1942 Dodge WC51. The military WC series 4x4s were powered by an in-line six-cylinder engine coupled to a four-speed transmission**

LEFT: **The WC52 Dodge 'weapons carrier' had a substantial winch mounted on the front bumper**

Chevrolet of Canada also produced trucks for the Allies including the C30 and the 1311X3.

Among other things GMC produced a vast number of the famous 6x6 'deuce and a half' 2.5ton trucks. These trucks were available in soft and hard-cab models with a cab not dissimilar in design to that of the CC Series half-ton trucks. Studebaker assembled almost 200,000 US6 2.5ton 6x4 and 6x6 trucks. Half of these went to the USSR as Lend Lease equipment. The GAZ plant in Gorky, Russia, produced a close copy of this truck in the post-war years. Studebaker also produced Wright Cyclone Flying Fortress engines and in excess of 15,000 Weasels, a light fully-tracked military vehicle that was designed by Studebaker's engineers.

LEFT: **A WC51 Dodge weapons carrier being unloaded from a landing barge by British and US personnel during the invasion of North Africa in November 1942**

Dodge was the US Army's main supplier of half-ton trucks and later its sole supplier of three-quarter-ton trucks during World War Two. It supplied more than 250,000 units until August 1945, for both the European and Pacific theatres of operations. The WC51/52 were the most common variants in the WC-series. Despite this WC was not an abbreviation of 'weapons carrier', but the general Dodge model code; W for 1941, and C for a nominal half-ton payload rating

RIGHT: US soldiers with a machine gun-equipped Willys MB Jeep during fighting in Germany in 1945

The tough and simple quarter-ton 4x4 Jeep became the most famous vehicle of World War Two. General George C. Marshall, US Army Chief of Staff during the war, and later U.S. Secretary of State, described the Jeep as 'America's greatest contribution to modern warfare'. News reporter Ernie Pyle once said, "It did everything. It went everywhere. Was a faithful as a dog, as strong as a mule, and as agile as a goat. It constantly carried twice what it was designed for and still kept going"

including the so-called 'waterfall' grille. It was so described because it comprised of a row of vertical bars.

In 1946 GMC resumed civilian production with light trucks that were almost identical to the pre-war models in order to give their staff time to design a new series of light trucks. IHC's civilian production also resumed fully in 1946, with the reintroduction of the K-series. These trucks were redesignated the KB-series with their redesign for 1947. Little had changed from the pre-war models and little would until 1950.

Following the cessation of hostilities Studebaker reintroduced its pre-war M-series trucks as 1946 and subsequently 1947 and 1948 models. As a result of the experience gained in wartime mass-production, in 1947 the company produced more than 67,000 trucks, a figure which exceeded the total of all the trucks the company had produced pre-war. Numerous variations of its 1942-type trucks were produced by Chevrolet from 1944-1945 and then in slightly revised forms in 1946.

The Dodge Power Wagon was a civilian version of the wartime WC-models, the model name being used on a variety of pickups from then on. Sales of Dodge trucks in this period were interesting; the years 1946 and 1947 were spectacular but there were drops in 1950 and 1953. Despite the otherwise increasing sales, the 1947 »

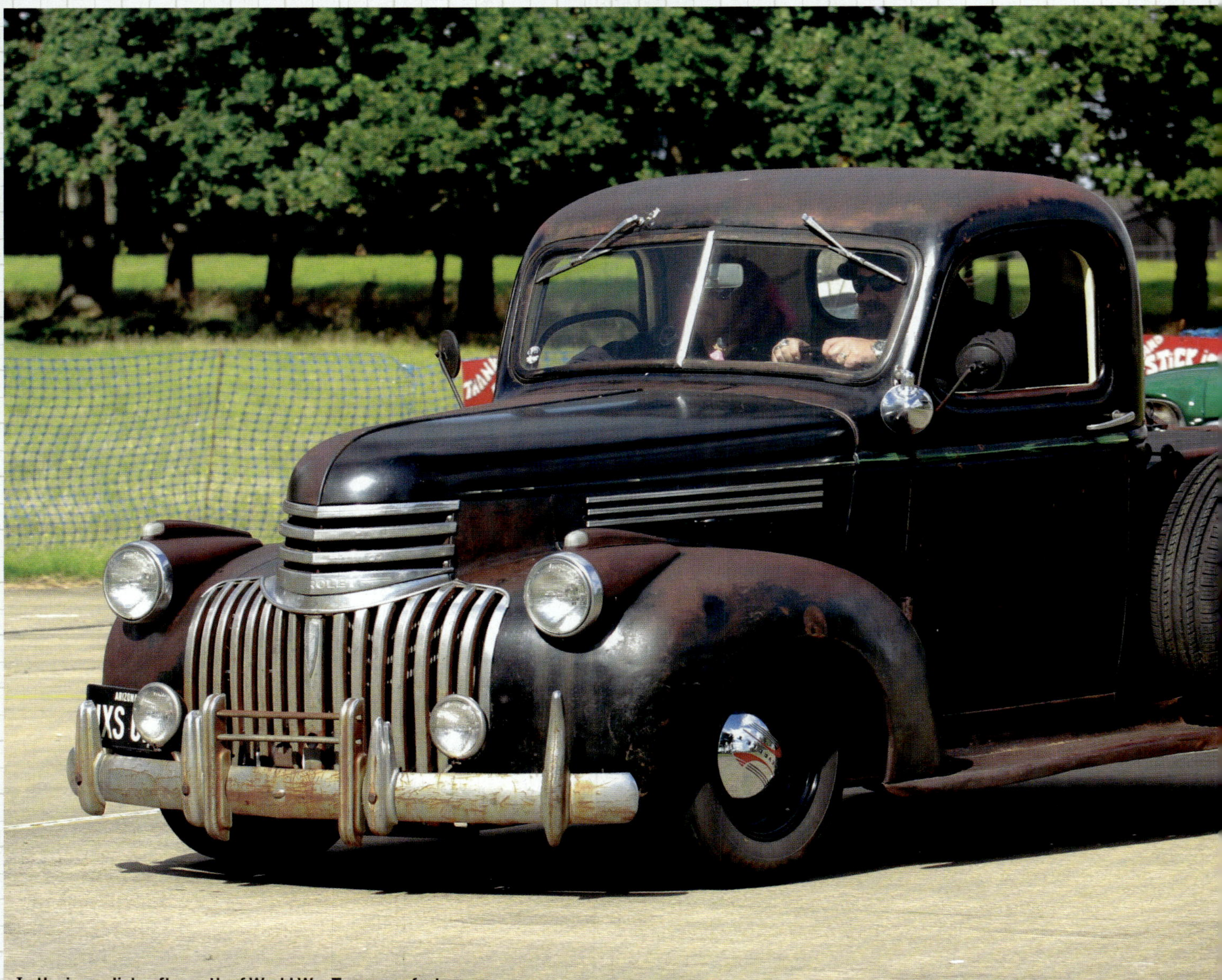

In the immediate aftermath of World War Two, manufacturers resumed production of pre-war pickups such as this '46/47 Chevy, to allow to allow time to develop new models

figures would not be surpassed until 1968 because of the sales decline of the late fifties. The company's market share fell to an all-time low in 1961 before seeing an upward trend.

The new post-war GMC models were to be the FC series that featured GMC's all new 'Advance Design' styling that had an overall appearance that was smooth and rounded. The grille comprised a series of horizontal bars and a GMC logo was affixed to the hood above the grille. The headlights were mounted in the fenders adding to the streamlined appearance. Underneath, the front suspension was redesigned. Due to the new design being introduced part way through 1947, it continued to be marketed through 1948. With only minor improvements, the design

RIGHT AND FAR RIGHT: **With only military production taking place from 1942 to 1945, the 1939 style trucks resumed production in 1946 and were largely unchanged through 1947. When sales resumed, they continued as the Dodge W-series. They were significant in Dodge history as the first trucks to be produced in the new, huge Warren, Michigan, plant.**

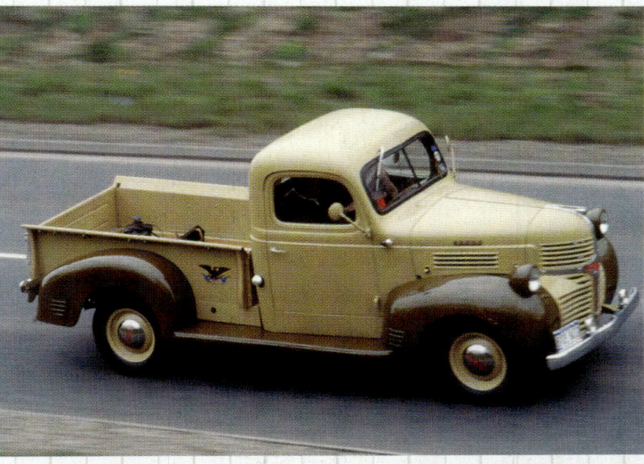

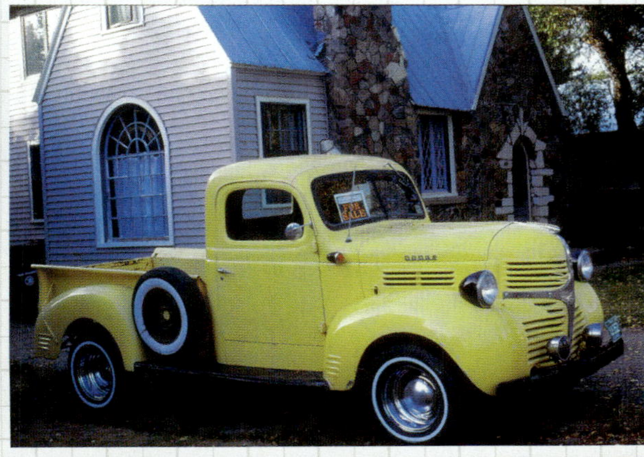

LEFT: After the war, Dodge developed the ¾-ton WC-series into the civilian 4×4 WDX one-ton Dodge Power Wagon for December 1946 onwards

LEFT, BELOW LEFT AND BELOW RIGHT: The Power Wagon adapted a closed civilian cab to a military chassis, using a military hood and radiator shell. It was powered by 230cid six-cylinder made about 95 hp and a four-speed transmission. Production ran until 1950

continued into 1949, the petrol tank now positioned inside the cab on all models. The half-ton FC-101 models were standard on a 116inch wheelbase and the range included a chassis, a chassis/cab, a pickup, a panel van, a canopy express and a suburban. »

RIGHT: Ford's immediate post-war trucks, like those from other automakers, used pre-war body styles such as this 1946 half-ton with the distinctive waterfall grille

The FC-102 models were also rated at a half-ton but based on a 125.25inch wheelbase. Also, on the 125.25inch wheelbase were the three-quarter ton FC-152 models. Both FC-102 and FC-152 models were available as chassis, chassis/cab, pickup and stake-bed models. For 1950 things continued pretty much unchanged although a few of the options were changed and the horsepower of the 228cid in-line six-cylinder engine was boosted slightly.

Chevrolet trucks were comprehensively redesigned for 1947 - also described by Chevrolet as the Advance-Design - now incorporated rear hinged hoods and a redesigned cab with such innovations as column shift. Sales generally boomed in the post-war years, Chevrolet selling

ABOVE AND RIGHT: On 1 May 1947 Chevrolet's all-new Advance-Design truck series that incorporated, what the manufacturer termed, the Unisteel cab, went into production

The grille of the new model comprised five horizontal bars that were topped by a hood ornament that contained the maker's name and the bowtie logo

as the F-2 and F-3 as a three-quarter tonner. The basic style endured through 1952 although the grille had been considerably redesigned for 1951.

The all-new post-war Dodges also appeared in 1948, the Series B models. The B-1-B was a half-ton, the B-1-C was a three-quarter ton and the B-1-D was a one-ton. The company made a number of upgrades and options available through the 1950s including automatic transmissions, column shifters, grilles, instrument panels as well as upgraded cab styling and even a variation on the cargo.

A new line of Studebaker trucks, referred to as the 2R series, appeared »

BELOW: By 1947 Willys was offering civilian versions of its wartime Jeep in the form of the CJ-2A as a quarter-ton truck that could be used like a smaller Power Wagon thanks to its opening tailgate and suitability for power take-offs

260,000 trucks in 1947. The new 1947 design was sequentially upgraded with vented windows, new door latches, a redesigned grille and new auto gearbox being introduced in 1951, 1952, and the last two in 1954 respectively. During this period Chevrolet offered half, three-quarter and one-ton pickups on 116, 125.25 and 137inch wheelbases respectively. In each capacity class pickups in the following configurations, chassis, chassis/cab, pickup, platform and stake bed were offered. In addition, there were half and one-ton panel vans and canopy wagons. The three series were designated 3100, 3600 and 3800 numbers, increasing with payload and wheelbase. These numerical designations continued for 1948, 1949 and into the fifties. While the overall appearance of the various models remained the same there were minor upgrades from model year to model year and increasing numbers of options; for example in 1950 options included rear view mirrors, new colour combinations, leather seats, a chrome radiator grille, deluxe equipment, spare wheel and tyre carrier, heavy duty radiator, dual tail lights, heavy duty rear springs, a school bus chassis, an oil bath air cleaner, heavy duty clutch, four-speed transmission, engine speed governor and numerous tyre options.

Ford's first new post-war range of trucks made the news in 1948 with the introduction of the F-series trucks, ranging from the half-ton F1 to the three-ton F-8. The F-series has, of course, endured for more than 70 years. For 1948 the styling had been altered radically from what had gone before and now the headlights were set into the recessed horizontally barred grille and the fenders were more squared off and joined across the top of the radiator grille below the hood. The cab was larger in all three dimensions than before and rubber mounted to the chassis. The new half-ton truck was known as the F-1 and available

Here's the chance you've waited for! Come in and drive a "Jeep." See for yourself how easily it rides and handles! Feel the mighty surge of power from its world-famous Willys-Overland "Jeep" Engine and the sure-footed thrust of "Jeep" 4-wheel-traction!

You'll see why the "Jeep" is the most useful and economical power vehicle on the farm... working the day around... the year around... saving you money because its cost is spread over so many farm jobs. You'll know why the "Jeep" can pull plows, harrows, mowers, etc., tow 5,500 lbs. and carry 800 lbs. You'll see how it can take you anywhere, on or off the road, in any weather. Examine the power take-off that furnishes up to 30 h.p., on the spot, to your shaft- and belt-driven equipment. You'll appreciate the convenience of the "Jeep" for running family errands.

Your Willys dealer invites you to come in now and drive a "Jeep."

Willys-Overland Motors, Inc., Toledo 1, Ohio

SEE THESE FEATURES THAT MAKE THE 'JEEP' A 4-FUNCTION VEHICLE

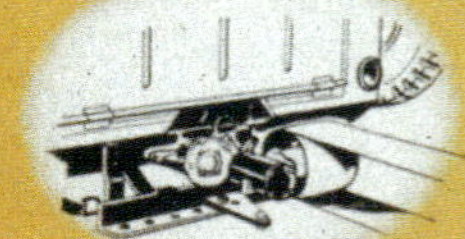

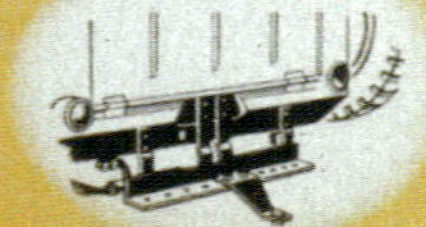

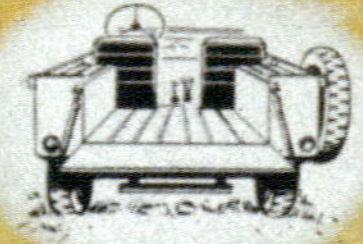

ABOVE AND BELOW: Alongside its Jeeps, from 1947, Willys was also manufacturing panel vans and trucks in both two and four-wheel-drive forms

RIGHT: The 1947 M5 Studebaker was similar to the 1946 and the pre-war models in appearance. During the war Studebaker had manufactured larger trucks, but resumed light truck production in early 1945

BELOW: Alongside its Power Wagon models, Dodge offered its regular pickup with different payloads including half, three-quarter, one-ton and 1.5 ton (pictured) as the WC, WD, WDX, WF models

ABOVE: Studebaker truck production continued almost unchanged into 1948. Model year production started in mid-1947 and continued until March 1948 when production was halted ahead of a new range of trucks for 1949

LEFT: The 1948 F-1 pickup was Ford's first new post-war design of truck. In a styling change the headlights were positioned in the recessed grille panel while the squared-off fenders and one-piece windscreen gave the truck a modern appearance

LEFT: The first-generation F-Series was a series of trucks produced by Ford from the 1948 through the 1952 model years. The introduction of the F-Series marked the divergence of Ford car and truck design with the use of a chassis intended specifically for F-1 trucks

RIGHT: Ford was the only company to offer V8 engines for both its pickup and medium duty trucks until 1954. Alongside pickup trucks, the model line included panel vans, bare and cowled chassis

BELOW LEFT AND BELOW RIGHT: Compared to the previous model of Ford trucks, the new F-1 cab was wider, offered increased headroom and included wider doors that were moved forward to improve access. The new frame, included a third cross-member which provided sufficient extra strength to be shared with Ford's F-2 to F-7 medium duty models

in 1949. There were half-ton 2R5 models, three-quarter ton 2R10 models and one-ton 2R15 models. These were of a completely new design, drawn by Robert Bourke and shared no sheet metal with Studebaker's car range. The 2R5 and 2R10 models used 112 and 122inch wheelbases respectively and were powered by six-cylinder engines. The trucks were assembled in the wartime plant that Studebaker had used to assemble aeroplane engines. It had been built by the US Government for war production and after the war Studebaker bought the plant and prepared it for truck production. The initial post-war sales boom didn't last long, before the end of the decade trucks were slow in moving off dealer's forecourts. To combat this, Studebaker instituted a year model registration procedure that meant a 1949 built truck could be registered as a 1950. This was a system not dissimilar to that employed by IHC and meant that the smaller manufacturers were not forced to compete with new lines from the bigger manufacturers each autumn.

Willys Overland was among the first to see the advantages that four-wheel-drive would offer a great number of commercial vehicle users and so offered a range of 4x4 pickups

RIGHT: Across the USA, Ford assembled F-Series trucks in 16 different factories from Michigan to California while, in Canada, Lincoln-Mercury sold the F-Series under the Mercury M-Series name

alongside its regular Jeeps. The trucks differed from Jeeps, but the design of the grille and front wings left no doubt as to which company had designed and manufactured them. The pickup trucks featured a closed-cab with a variety of rear body types being available including a step-side, a stake bed and a chassis cab for specialist equipment to be installed on the back. The pickup range was complemented by a line of panel vans and estate car models. The four-wheel-drive models were capable of mounting power take offs to drive machinery. The first 4x4 truck from Willys rolled off the Toledo, Ohio production line in February 1948 and trucks continued to do so until 1963, with only minor improvements along the way. The grille was slightly redesigned and a one-piece windscreen substituted for the two-piece item originally used. Until the 1950s 4x4 pickups from the major US manufacturers would remain something of a novelty though. ★

Stake-bed F-1 pickups were one of seven half-ton models marketed with a 114inch wheelbase chassis and a choice of six-cylinder or V8 engines

The Fabulous
FIFTIES

In January 1950 a completely new range of trucks - the L-series - was unveiled by IHC. Both restyled and re-engineered they now incorporated wide, flat fenders, a less rounded hood and significant changes to both the radiator grille and trim. Under the hood was a new in-line six-cylinder overhead valve engine. This style ran until 1953 when it would be superseded by the R-series, a development of the L-series. The front end was again redesigned and became concave with an oval aperture. A two-tone paint job

was an option, as was a model with a greater payload. The standard half-ton pickups were known as the R-100 and had a 115inch wheelbase while the R-102 was the heavier truck with the same wheelbase. The R-110 was the longer wheelbase variant, also available as the R-111 and R-112. These trucks were to remain in production until 1955 when the S-series would make its debut. The 1949 2R truck was a good seller for Studebaker so few changes were made for 1950, 1951, 1952 or the final year of 2R production in 1953. At GMC it was a similar story for 1951, 1952 and 1953 as only minor changes were made leading up to the major redesign for 1955.

War in Korea

The Korean War started on 25 June 1950 when North Korean soldiers invaded South Korea by crossing the 38th Parallel, the line at which the country had been arbitrarily partitioned in 1945. In response to the outbreak, the US Department of Defence reactivated the Ordnance Tank Automotive Center in Detroit, Michigan, with a view to again mobilise the automotive industry for war production. On 15 January 1951 Dodge began building trucks for a military contract for example. Most of the automakers had received military contracts of one sort or another but in excess of eight million cars, trucks and buses were produced in the USA in 1950, estimated to be more than 75% of all the vehicles made in the world that year. The Korean War continued into 1951 as the People's Republic of China sent troops and assistance »

The Chevrolet Advance-Design trucks were gradually upgraded. In late 1949, the hood side emblems were changed to numbers that designate cargo capacity; 3100 for half-ton, 3600 for three-quarter-ton and 3800 for one-ton. In 1950, telescopic shock absorbers replaced the lever-action type and it was the last year for the driver's side cowl vent. New serial number codes were introduced HP, HR and HS for half, three-quarter and one-ton respectively. From 1951, the doors gained vent quarter windows. In 1952, the outer door handles were changed to the push button type. 1953 was the last year for the 216cid inline-six engine while hood side emblems now read 3100, 3600, 3800, 4400, or 6400 new serial number codes are introduced; H, J and L across the three payloads

to the communist North Koreans. In order to avoid raising the stakes too high President Truman was forced to sack General MacArthur, the UN Commander in Chief when he talked of invading China. This escalation led to restrictions on the amount of certain metals including zinc, chromium, tin and nickel that could be used by the American auto industry for work other than that related to defence. Chrysler and Cadillac were making tanks and GMC truck plants were assembling the M-135 6x6 truck for the US Army. Numerous other restrictions also came into force as a result, the National Production Agency (NPA) limiting both car and truck production in order to ensure a continuous flow of equipment for the war. The NPA assigned a quota of trucks to each manufacturer based on their percentage market share. Dodge's NPA quota, for example, was 13% of the industry total.

LEFT: **The model's popularity has endured among enthusiasts. This sleek example is a recent custom take on the stepside version**

The Korean War dragged on through 1952, the year that Republican Dwight D. Eisenhower was elected president »

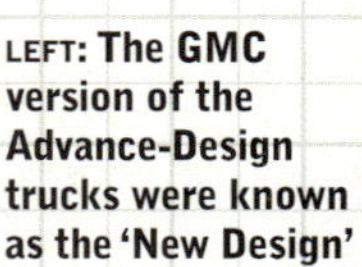

LEFT: **The GMC version of the Advance-Design trucks were known as the 'New Design'**

BELOW LEFT: **The 1951 GMC 253-22/24 was a 137inch wheelbase, one-ton version of the trucks in the comprehensive GMC line that included chassis-cabs and stake beds**

BELOW RIGHT: **For 1952, Dodge carried over its B-series pickups from the previous year. The half-ton pictured was the B-3-B while larger capacity models were the B-3-C and B-3-D for three-quarter and one-ton respectively**

RIGHT: For 1951 Ford pickups, the grille was restyled to comprise a large horizontal bar and three vertical bars that moved the headlights further apart. It was painted either ivory or argent, with either painted or chrome headlight trims while the hood trim was also redesigned

RIGHT: Where specified, a V8 emblem was fitted to the curved panel above the grille opening. The cab featured several revisions including a larger rear window and updated door panels and pickup trucks' tailgate was redesigned and a hardwood floor introduced

and ended only after the agreement at Panmunjon in July 1953. The cost had been high including 51,000 American dead and the face of world politics changing again. The war had been the first confrontation of the big powers in the nuclear age and was the model for the brinkmanship of numerous Cold War era conflicts to come.

The F-series trucks carried Ford into the 1950s on a very firm footing with Ford becoming the nation's number two automaker, partially as a result of a

RIGHT: This F-1 has had its grille customised with the addition of extra vertical parts. It has the V8 logo and the grille and trims are all chromed to complement the metallic paintwork

more modern appearance than that which had gone before. It was available in a great number of variants, of which were the one-ton models, available as platform and stake trucks, step-sides and as the F10D3 straight-six powered unit or the F10R3 which was the V8-powered version. Larger capacity versions were the three-quarter-ton F-250 and F-350. Larger again was the F-500. As was by now the norm, the basic design would last several years with only minor upgrades in terms of grille changes, body panel variations, interior changes and similar.

Innovation in the form of factory 4x4s came from Ford in the 1950s. These trucks were also introduced »

serious labour dispute at Chrysler. The F-series underwent a redesign in 1951 when a redesigned grille was fitted. In 1952 two new overhead valve engines were made available, an in-line six and a V8. The major facelift however was saved for 1953 and Ford's Golden Anniversary, the most major redesign in two decades. Most significant from the truck buyer's point of view was that the F-series was given the three-digit designations that have been used ever since. The F-1 became the F-100, the F-2 and F-3 became the F-250 and the F-4, slightly downgraded, became the F-350. This seems straightforward but there were, with the numerous options, a total of 194 models in the Ford truck range. The F-100 as the new model was officially known or 'Effie', as it soon became referred to, was introduced on 13 March 1953, with a sleeker and

ABOVE: The three-quarter-ton F-2 and F-3 models featured a 96inch bed on a 122inch wheelbase in pickup and panel truck versions

LEFT: The larger capacity models were the F-5 and F-6 of 1.5 and two-tons respectively. These were offered as a conventional medium-duty pickup and as the B-series for bus chassis and the Cab Over Engine (COE) configuration truck (pictured)

Willys-Overland Jeep 4x4 truck. Shortly after introducing the CJ Jeep, that was essentially a civilianised version of the wartime Jeep, Willys-Overland introduced its larger 4x4 pickup. Available in half-ton, panel-van and one-ton pickup forms, the truck was powered by a 63-hp L-head four-cylinder engine with production running from 1947–1965 and, while modern when first produced, the nameless pickup was stale by 1965 its final year

in response to rumours emanating from Chevrolet about that company's own 4x4. International Harvester introduced its first 4x4 pickup, the R-series, in 1953. It followed this in late 1955 when the company, then the third largest pickup truck manufacturer in the US, brought out the S-series of trucks including the 4x4 S-120 model. There were 13 variations of this truck with four different wheelbases, chassis-cabs, stake beds and platform trucks.

Ford, GMC and Chevrolet continued to offer 4x4 trucks, usually in the form of a four-wheel-drive variant of an existing truck. Ford's first contenders for a section of this growing market were the 1956 F-100 and F-250. 4x4 models were available as both pickups and chassis-cabs.

Dodge built the second series of its Power Wagon, the serious 4x4 working truck from 1951-56. Based on the military vehicles it had

supplied during World War Two, it was considered the undisputed king off the highway in America's backwoods. The Power Wagon found favour for logging and oil exploration and on wilderness construction sites such as remote dam projects. Power Wagons were available with a variety of bodies and all were built by Chrysler's Dodge Truck Division and briefly marketed under the Desoto and

Fargo names. Fargo was a brand of trucks originally produced in the US by the Fargo Motor Car Company. Chrysler absorbed Dodge and eventually Fargo trucks became rebadged Dodges, similar to the parallel sale or 'badge engineering' by General Motors of its GMC and Chevrolet truck lines.

The comprehensive nature of the new model range in 1953 represented a huge investment from the Ford Motor Company so changes were minimal until 1956 when Ford was again forced to act as a result of the introduction, by major rival Chevrolet, of new and competitive products during 1955. Ford innovated in the still up and coming area of vehicle safety with tubeless tyres, safety steering wheel, better door locks and a shatterproof rear-view mirror. Ironically these inexpensive upgrades failed as a sales incentive but just a decade later government regulations would force such measures on the US automotive industry.

The 1954 American test the first aerial H-bomb at Bikini Atoll also coincided with something that would later affect »

ABOVE: The 2R5 and later 3R5 series half-ton trucks were equipped with 6.5-foot boxes, the three-quarter-ton models used eight-foot boxes, and all could be purchased as a cab and chassis or with a stake bed. This 2R5 has a later grille fitted

LEFT: Like its rivals Studebaker offered its early '50s trucks in half and three-quarter-ton forms, as well as larger payload trucks such as this 1950 duallie

ABOVE LEFT AND ABOVE RIGHT: The International L-series was introduced by International Harvester in the autumn of 1949 and would continue to be produced it until 1952. Three wheelbases and a choice of three six-cylinder engines were offered. This is a 1952 L-110 with a 115inch wheelbase

RIGHT: The second generation of the Ford F-Series trucks was produced by Ford for the 1953 to 1956 model years. To emphasise the update, the model designation was changed from F-1 to three numbers, such as F-100, something that has remained in use on F-Series trucks until the present day

America's future. The agreement that partitioned Vietnam into North and South and recognised both Cambodia and Laos as independent nations, following the end of French rule in what was formerly French Indochina. The mid-1950s Federal programme of Interstate and Freeway building within the US also caused a shift in the buying patterns for trucks. Demand increased for higher performance trucks and meant that the large displacement in-line six and V8-powered models became ever more popular.

The all-new GMC and Chevrolet ranges of 1955 model trucks were

RIGHT: A 1953 F-100 with a 239ci flathead V8 engine. A straight-six option was available and the grille would be slightly redesigned for subsequent model years

supposed to go on sale alongside the redesigned car line in the autumn of 1954, but the scale of Chevrolet's model line revision, sales pressures from Ford and Korean War contracts, forced the company to delay the introduction until April 1955. The first series of 1955 trucks were slightly upgraded 1954 models that were on sale from August 1954 until March 1955. The first 1955 series incorporated two immediately apparent changes, the grille and windshield. The grille was changed from having a series of horizontal bars to a single heavier central bar and a single vertical bar, Chevrolet being stamped into the horizontal bar. The windshield became a single piece item, with the interior of the trucks redesigned with a revised

ABOVE: **This 1953 Ford F-100 was customised with painted flames and alloy slot mags in California during the 1970s and has survived that way ever since**

LEFT: **This 1953 Ford F-100 wears a patinated paintwork finish that is currently very popular**

steering wheel and dash arrangement. Less obvious was the new-style load bed for pickup variants, that was lower at the sides but deeper overall. The three-speed transmission was beefed up and a Hydra-Matic auto gearbox was added to the options list. The designations of 3100, 3600 and 3800 continued although some years earlier the 3700 had already been added for the Dubl-Duty models.

The Chevy trucks that would become legendary however, were introduced as the second series redesign for 1955 albeit using the 3100 series designations. The new trucks featured wrap-around windshields, redesigned fenders »

LEFT: **Chevy's Advance-Design trucks that had been introduced in 1947 received their first major restyle in 1954. This included fitting a triple row of large horizontal grille bars bisected by a central vertical bar, with parking lights incorporated in the grille. They also matched the corresponding GMC model trucks**

RIGHT: The design life of the 1954 Chevrolet Series 3100 half-ton pickups spanned less than two years, making the trucks relatively rare today. This one has aftermarket alloy slot mag wheels fitted

RIGHT: The cargo box was changed for 1954, with higher walls and a flat, instead of sloping, top rail. Mechanically, the 235.5-cid six was virtually a new engine, with higher compression, new bearings, and high-pressure lubrication. Torque-tube drive was retained and Hydra-matic transmission was an extra-cost option

and truck beds and had the option of a V8 engine. The 3100 was the half-ton commercial while the 3200 was a half-ton on a longer wheelbase, the 3600 was the three-quarter-ton and the 3800 the one-ton. The Dubl-Duty models used 3400, 3500, 3700 for its various models. A cameo pickup model appeared as a limited edition and the new design would endure with minor upgrades until the restyled model of 1958 was unveiled with dual headlamps. Chevrolet had introduced the new models with what it described as 'taskforce' styling that included new features such as the panoramic windscreen that wrapped around the corners of the cab, the flatter bonnet, wing and roofline as well as the egg-crate grille. The trucks were only slightly upgraded for 1956 and would subsequently be upgraded for 1957 in a similarly minor way.

The new GMC trucks were also considerably more angular than their predecessors. The front end featured a two-bar grille reminiscent of passenger cars of the era and was complemented by hooded headlamps and a massive chromed bumper. The GMC logo was mounted on the lower portion of the hood front in a stylised form. The »

ABOVE: International was the last manufacturer to offer an all-new post-war pickup. Revised models, the R-Series (pictured) trucks were introduced in late 1953, featuring subtle refinements including a new radiator grille

LEFT: Dodge Powerwagon production continued through the 1950s with numerous upgrades including new cab and ran alongside production of other Dodge pickups

LEFT: In 1954, Dodge launched its modernised, job-rated trucks but the manufacturer was judicious when it came to changing much from the previous model, however, all the front sheet-metal was totally new. Visually, the biggest changes were a one-piece windshield, and a new trapezoid-shaped grille opening with a pair of horizontal floating bars

The largest payload versions were the 'Big Job' F-700, F-750, F-800, and F-900 model series. The cabover engine versions were the C-series like this C-750

ABOVE: The 1955 Ford F-100 pickup is distinguished by the V-shaped dip in the upper grille bar

RIGHT: The 1953-56 Ford F-100 was also available as the Model 82 panel van

BELOW: Larger payload versions of the Ford F-100 pickup were the medium-duty 1.5-ton F-500 and the two-ton F-600 with the same cab, pictured

ABOVE: In recent years, the once unpopular classic cabover trucks have gained popularity as the basis of stylish car transporters

BELOW LEFT AND BELOW RIGHT: The 1956 F-100 is a one-year only body style and is easily identified as it has vertical windshield pillars and a wrap-around windshield as opposed to the sloped pillars and angled windshield of the 1953-55 models

cab was redesigned to incorporate a wraparound windshield and the higher front fender line ran right through the cab and doors. The comprehensive range of new designs were variously designated as Series 100, 102, 150, 251, 252, 253 models reflecting wheelbases and payloads. The trucks fitted with the optional V8 were given an additional '8' suffix. In this way the half-ton model on a 114inch wheelbase was a Model 100 while the V8 variant was the 100-8. The Series 150-8 trucks were three-quarter-ton trucks on a 123.25inch wheelbase and V8-powered. Of these various models, 84,877 vehicle registrations »

The 1953-56 F-100 is one of the most popular classic trucks for several reasons not least the fact that it is a stylish vehicle that is suited to various finishes and custom treatments. The 1954 F-100 was the last year to use the flathead engine in the US. The 1954-55 models saw the introduction of the new 239ci overhead valve Y-block V8, while the six-cylinder engine's displacement was increased from 215 to 223ci. In succeeding years, the Y-block was replaced with the bigger capacity 256, 272 and 312ci versions. Power steering was an optional extra, as was a larger wraparound back window for the 1956 models

were made for the 1955 calendar year. The 1956 GMC models continued almost unchanged from the 1955 ones, although the V8 models were no longer listed as a separate series, the V8 simply became an option. The engines were increased in displacement to 269.5 and 316.6cid for the six and eight-cylinder units respectively. A redesigned grille was the only obvious styling change for 1957 but for 1958 the range was redesigned in several small ways and a wide-side steel pickup body »

RIGHT: The 1956 international Harvester S-120 4x4 was an update of the late-1955 R-120 4x4, with the same styling changes as on the rest of the light duty S-models. The six-cylinder BD-240 engine was standard and three or four-speed transmissions were offered

RIGHT: In March 1955, Chevrolet's 'Task Force' series trucks replaced the Advance-Design model, as it redesigned the truck line for the second half of 1955. The newer design became known as the 2nd Series and the 3100 was the half-ton offered in pickup and panel van configurations

BELOW LEFT: The truck's signature wraparound 'Sweep-Sight' windshield and stepside truck bed make a '50s Task Force truck instantly recognisable. Fenders have single headlights and a one-piece emblem is mounted below the horizontal line on the fender

BELOW RIGHT: Two iconic American classics; a 1955 Chevrolet pickup tows an Airstream caravan

windshield superseded the two-piece item used until then. For 1955 styling changes were kept to a minimum but numerous upgrades were made to the power train of the trucks. Because of these changes, including the use of an overhead valve V8 in some models, the trucks were again redesignated, this time as the E-series. There were E5 and E7 half-ton trucks and E10 and E12 three-quarter-tonners, the E7 and E12 models were the V8-powered versions. The V8 models proved popular and helped Studebaker achieve a good sales total for the year. In October 1954 Studebaker had merged with Packard but it was not really to either company's

was introduced. Less decorative hub caps, dual headlights and a new grille changed the exterior appearance.

During this period, it was not just Ford, GMC and Chevrolet that were redesigning their trucks to tempt customers. Studebaker's range of trucks were redesignated the 3R series for 1954 and given a minor facelift. Much of the sheet-metal was the same, although the grille was redesigned and a curved one-piece

advantage and by 1956 Studebaker had lost money for each of the years since the merger. This meant that the money was not available for the complete redesign of the truck range. A new name - Transtar - and a minor redesign

denote Anniversary. The styling was modern and angular and the trucks came with a choice of bed styles; the custom pickup, the pickups that were effectively fleetside and stepside models respectively. The fleetside type bed was constructed using the rear fenders of the IHC Travelall station wagon. For 1959 the range of trucks were designated the B-series that were the previous year's A-series models with minor updates including quad headlamps and a chromed car-like grille. This range was to be carried over into 1960 with the only major change being that a V8 engine was now standard equipment. Ford's next overall styling change was made in 1957 and in the same year the Ford Ranchero made its debut. This new truck combined car and truck features to offer a car-type cab and front sheet-metal with a pickup load bed between the rear fenders. Similar models continued through 1958 and 1959 although in the latter »

was all that was done. Sales were not as good as hoped so Studebaker truck production was moved back to the main Studebaker plant and the wartime plant leased to another company. Studebaker then began to make annual changes to its model line and alongside the Transtar introduced a basic pickup known as the Scotsman. It was the lowest priced pickup on sale in the USA in 1958.

The IHC S-series of trucks were made from late 1955 until mid-1957. The design was apparently refined from the R-series, although they had a more square appearance partially as a result of the headlights being mounted high on the fenders rather than previously within the confines of the radiator grille. The windshield also had been redesigned to increase visibility. Options of payloads continued and a variety of optional interiors were made available. At this time IHC held third position in terms of US sales and again announced new models in late 1957. The next major restyle from Dodge came in 1957 when the front end was restyled and the Sweptside D100 was introduced, larger capacity V8s - 315cid - were fitted and even the utilitarian Power Wagon was redesigned although the original style model was still available. The redesigned cabs featured a one-piece rear hinged hood and were changed slightly for the next year when double headlights were fitted.

IHC considered 1957 to be its 50th year in truck manufacture and brought out anniversary models to mark the occasion. The range of trucks which had been significantly redesigned were designated the A-series to

Classic custom trucks have been a hugely popular part of the street rod hobby for decades. There's no question that Chevrolet's 'Tri-Five' trucks from the 1955, 1956, and 1957 model years, are favourites within that scene. The mid-fifties was the era when Chevrolet and every other manufacturer was modernising the lines of their cars, their designers appling the same imagination to the pickups, giving them a stylish, outward appearance. Their popularity has endured as one of the most popular truck styles for almost 70 years since. Solid trucks can still be found and the sky is the limit in terms of what can be done in terms of bodywork and chassis and performance upgrades, as this selection show

year the base model Ranchero was discontinued leaving only the top of the range Custom Ranchero available.

Little Rock, Arkansas

The latter years of the 1950s were banner years for truck manufacturers but seriously troubled in other ways. In 1957 President Eisenhower was trying to enforce racially integrated schools in Little Rock, Arkansas. The crisis erupted when a Federal District Court decreed that nine black students should be allowed to enrol in the previously segregated Central High School. Orville Fabus, the segregationist Governor of Arkansas went as far as mobilising the National Guard to block the school to the new students. Eisenhower ensured

FAR LEFT AND LEFT: In 1957, GMC introduced its model line known as the GMC Blue Chip 'Money-Maker' line that attracted customers to the brand. The 1955-1957 truck line had been designed to give drivers the some of the best-looking trucks available. GMC's 1957 models featured fresh styling features such as a wrap-around rear window and panoramic windshield with a deep centre steering wheel

LEFT: The third-generation of the Ford F-Series trucks were produced by Ford from 1957-1960. Following the style of competitors at Dodge and GMC, Ford widened the front bodywork to integrate the cab, front fenders and hood into the bodywork with a clamshell design in front of the wraparound windshield

ABOVE: The first light duty-style Power Wagons were introduced in 1957 with the introduction of the four-wheel-drive versions of the Dodge C-Series pickups and Town Wagons. From 1957, half-ton 4x2s were D100s and 4x4s were W100s, three-quarter-ton 4x2 and 4x4 were the D200 and W200 respectively. All used the same cabs and front sheet-metal and cargo boxes. The two-ton W500 Power Wagon (only a chassis cab was built) was introduced in 1956 as the C3-HW

FAR LEFT: At the rear, two types of pickup boxes were now offered; the traditional separate-fendered box was dubbed 'Flareside', while boxes (pictured) that integrated the pickup bed, cab, and front fenders were 'Styleside'

the withdrawal of the National Guard and had to send US paratroopers to Little Rock to ensure the they got into school.

The 1958 Chevrolet Apache used the same basic cab as the previous Chevrolet truck models but featured a redesigned hood, grille and fenders. The fenders incorporated double headlamps and the trim was redesigned. The stepside bed continued, although later in the year Chevrolet offered what they termed the Fleetside bed which was more like the smooth sides of the Cameo models, but fabricated in steel. A four-wheel-drive transmission was available as an option. The basic styling continued until the new for 1960 trucks were unveiled in the autumn of 1959. As was usual the basic model was upgraded and offered with slightly different options each year. The El Camino was brand new for 1959 and was seen in many ways as a car and truck hybrid. It combined contemporary car front styling and a truck bed between the styled rear fenders. In this same year Chevrolet began to use the C10-C30 model designations that are still in use.

The end of the 1950s saw the sands of time shifting again; Sputnik, the world's first satellite had gone into orbit in 1957, so beginning the »

The Jeep 4x4 Forward Control was a truck produced by Willys Motors, latterly Kaiser Jeep, from 1956 to 1965. Introduced in 1956, FC-150 model was based on the 4x4 CJ-5 Jeep with its 81 in wheelbase, pictured

BELOW AND RIGHT: The 1957-58 Studebaker 3E series was made while Studebaker was in dire financial straits so invested little its truck products. For the 1956 and 1957-58 models, all Studebaker trucks were called 'Transtar'

RIGHT: From 1958 all Chevrolet's light-duty trucks were called 'Apache'. This accompanied a significant redesign of the front end and grille that contained parking lights. Four headlights were installed instead of the previous two. The hood remained similar to 1955/1956 models, but with a flat central portion

RIGHT: For 1959 new style-side all-steel bed replaces the Cameo version and was called 'Fleetside' by Chevrolet and 'Wideside' by GMC. It was available in 78 and 96inch lengths. There were minimal changes from 1958, the most apparent was a larger and more ornate hood emblem and redesigned badging on the fenders

space age. In recognition of the fact that such new technology would no doubt have a place in the automobile industry, various manufacturers produced futuristic vehicles. GMC's truck and coach division rolled out the Turbo-Titan, an experimental truck designed and built to use a gas turbine engine for power. Ford produced the similarly experimental Glidaire that travelled on a cushion of air rather than wheels. They took the idea a step further and followed the Glidaire with the Levacar that, like the Curtiss-Wright Aircar, was also an air-cushion vehicle. By 1959 Chevrolet, as part of GMC, produced the Turbo Titan II, a second gas turbine powered truck and Chrysler experimented with an electro-chemical source of power, while Cadillac experimented with radar for cars. Also hinting at future developments was the fact that 1957 was the year that saw the first imported VW trucks and vans take to America's highways. ★

BELOW: The Apache's greatest asset was its V8 engine. While the 235ci straight-six remained the base option, the Apache received its first V8 the same year as Chevrolet's passenger cars, enabling it to compete with the Ford F-100 that had OHV V8-power from 1954

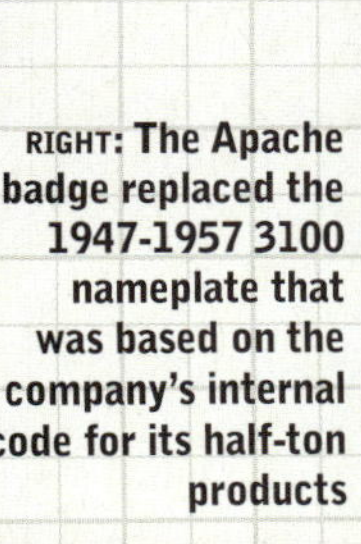

RIGHT: The Apache badge replaced the 1947-1957 3100 nameplate that was based on the company's internal code for its half-ton products

ABOVE LEFT: The entire 1955-59 Chevrolet truck models are usually considered as 'Task Force' trucks but the Apache name designates the quad-headlamp models introduced for 1958. It was successful enough that when the first of the new C/K-series trucks debuted for 1960, Chevrolet continued the Western-themed name on the next generation

ABOVE MIDDLE: The Chevrolet El Camino was a coupé utility vehicle, produced by Chevrolet between 1959–60. Unlike other Chevrolet pickups, the El Camino was adapted from the standard two-door Chevrolet station wagon platform

ABOVE RIGHT: In 1959 the Ford F-100 remained Ford's entry level half-ton truck. It was available with a 78inch load bed on a 110inch wheelbase chassis, or 96inch on 118inch chassis. The load bed, as in previous years, was offered in a still-traditional Flareside (pictured) or Styleside configurations. The general styling had carried over from 1958, but the facelift for '59 provided styling changes including the redesigned hood with Ford in block letters, bumper and grille

ABOVE: GMC and Chevrolet trucks were virtually identical except for the grilles and nameplates, although the differences have varied over the years. From 1955 through 1959 light duty GMC trucks with V8s were fitted with Pontiac, Buick, and Oldsmobile V8s while Canadian-built trucks used Chevrolet engines. GMC had its own line of in-line, six-cylinder engines from 1939-1959. Chevrolet trucks were marketed towards private ownership, while GMC was focused towards commercial uses

The Ford Ranchero was a coupe utility produced by Ford from 1957 onwards. Like the El Camino, the Ranchero was adapted from a two-door station wagon platform that integrated the cab and cargo bed into the body

ABOVE: This type of truck bed is slab-sided, and the wheel arches are contained within the bed. Wideside is how GMC described it while Chevrolet used the term 'Fleetside,' while other brands have their own terminology including 'Townside' by Jeep and 'Sweptline' by Dodge. Currently, Fleetside seems to be the most popular term used across the brands for this style of truck bed

There have long been 4x4 pickups made by automakers which have become an essential part of each manufacturer's line up. However, a style of custom truck that has been popular since the 1990s is to fit classic 1950s pickup bodywork onto the chassis and mechanical components of a later 4x4 such as a Chevy Blazer, to get a sky-high hot rod as these pictures illustrate

THE SIXTIES
The Space Age

As the 1960s opened, the Dan Dare spaceship-style fins were still to be seen on the rear fenders of many American sedans with hints of similar styling appearing on trucks, as the USA accounted for almost 48% of worldwide automobile production. The early years of the 1960s were troubled ones for the American nation. On 9 November 1960 Democrat John F. Kennedy was elected US President. On 22 December 1961 James Davis from Tennessee became the first American serviceman killed in Vietnam and less than a month later on 12 January Operation Ranch Hand took place to defoliate parts of Vietnam using the chemical Agent Orange.

The Bay of Pigs fiasco and the Cuban Missile Crisis followed as Cold War tensions heightened. In the south racial tensions also heightened when in 1963 a number of black civil rights workers were murdered in Alabama and Mississippi. George Wallace the segregationist Governor of Alabama mobilised the Alabama National Guard to prevent two black students from taking their places at the University of Alabama in Tuscaloosa. In almost

ABOVE: The Ford F-100 had been attractively restyled for 1959 and ran into 1960, albeit with further styling changes. This was the only generation of the F-Series trucks that used quad headlamps and for 1960 a Ford emblem in place of the word Ford was positioned between vents on the leading edge of the hood

a repeat of the Arkansas crisis, the Alabama National Guard had to be wrested from control of the state by the president. In August 1963 Martin Luther King made his historic speech at the Lincoln Memorial in Washington DC and in November President Kennedy was assassinated in Dallas, Texas. Lyndon Baines Johnson, the Vice-President who was with Kennedy on the trip to Texas, was sworn in as the 35th US president in Dallas.

The 1960s got off to a good start for Chevrolet when it became America's number one truck maker »

LEFT AND ABOVE: The 1960 F-600 was one of the larger payload versions of the F-100 that included one-ton F-350s and up. As this one, equipped with a post hole borer, illustrates the F-600 was available as a chassis-cab intended for specialist work applications

ABOVE AND RIGHT: A 1960 Dodge D100 stepwise pickup powered by a 318ci V8 with a factory upgrade four-speed transmission. Dodge offered both this stepside version with its 'utiline' 78inch short bed and its flush-sided 'Sweptside' load bed

RIGHT: The 1960 model year was pivotal for General Motors' light trucks. The market for pickups was booming and the emphasis on styling, comfort, and power was stronger than ever as all major manufacturers vied for a piece of this expanding pie. The evolution of the Chevrolet Task Force and GMC Blue Chip trucks helped popularise many features that are standard specification today, including fleetside boxes, V-8 engines, automatic transmissions and comfortable interiors

in 1961, albeit by the narrow margin of only 3670 trucks ahead of Ford. Chevrolet's production equated to a 30.39% market share. The C10 was one of a series of 185 trucks made by the company in 1960. Such a large number was achieved by the manufacture of a number of different wheelbases as well as a number of optional engines and transmissions. The K-prefix models were 4x4 variants of the C-series. The trucks had been redesigned to include a redesigned grille with repositioned headlamps. The fenders, body sides and hood were also redesigned with a sculpted line down either side of the body. The range included the half-ton Series 1000, the three-quarter-ton commercial and Dubl-Duti Series 2000 models and the one-ton Series 3000 models. Minor styling changes took the line into 1961 and a restyled hood took it forward into 1962. The styling changes were kept to a minimum for 1963 but a coil sprung front suspension arrangement was introduced at the same time on the 4x2 C-series trucks. Chevrolet truck number eight million was produced in 1962 and the El Camino appeared as a mid-size pickup similar in configuration to the Chevelle automobile. Production at Chevrolet's plants was in full swing and a further million trucks had been produced by 1964.

Ford had entered the 1960s with another redesign for the popular F-series trucks in 1961 that included a reproportioned body. By now it had single headlights, a horizontally barred grille and a wraparound windshield. This design lasted several years into

As was the norm for the big manufacturers, the light-duty cab sheet-metal was used across the range of the payload models but only as chassis-cab and stake models as this 1.5 ton GMC 3000 shows

the 1960s, through a number of minor upgrades such as the facelift for 1962 and new grilles for 1964 and 1965. The wheelbase was lengthened, while the front overhang was shortened. In 1964 the Ford name was pressed into the tailgate and long bed variants of the F-100 and the F-150 appeared aimed at those who wanted to fit camper shells.

The results of a GMC redesign appeared in 1960 when the company's trucks were given a more modern looking cab that had a lower overall

$650 extra and three payloads of truck were available. The P1000 series were the half ton models while the P1500 and P2500 were the three-quarter and one-ton models respectively. The choice of body types across these ranges including chassis/cab, pickup, stake-bed, panel, wideside and fenderside models. As GMC did not produce trucks on a strict model year by model year basis the range did not necessarily change in the autumn of each year, ≫

ABOVE: The Jeep Forward Control truck was produced by Kaiser Jeep until 1965 and primarily marketed as work vehicles for corporate, municipal and civilian use. It was also assembled in other international markets

LEFT: The first generation of the C/K series was a range of trucks that was manufactured by General Motors for the 1960 to 1966 model years. They were the first General Motors pickups on a dedicated truck platform and included pickups, chassis-cabs as well as medium and heavy commercial trucks

FAR LEFT: Alongside pickup trucks, the new C/K light truck line was the basis of the fifth generation of the GMC Carryall that was marketed as both a truck-based wagon (pictured) and a panel van

height than previously. A concave styling feature ran along the sides of the fenders, cab and bed. The full width hood had lights in pods on either side while the headlights were dual and mounted in the grille. The rear of the cab featured an overhang while the front included a wraparound windshield. Underneath the trucks were also a number of new features including a new front suspension system, a redesigned frame that was both stronger and lighter and an optional V6 engine of 305 cubic inch displacement. Four-wheel-drive was an option at

LEFT: A 1961 Ford F-100 awaiting restoration and a new lease of life

RIGHT: A postcard produced to promote the 1962 Ford F-100 Styleside. Dealers sent these postcards to existing customers to entice them trade up to the new models

RIGHT AND BELOW: For the 1960 model year Chevrolet had introduced a new body style of light pick-up truck that incorporated a number of firsts. Most important of these was a drop-centre ladder frame, allowing the cab to sit lower, and independent front suspension, giving an almost car-like ride in a truck. The 1960, 1961 and 1962 (pictured) models used torsion bar front suspension with trailing arm suspension rear

to dual headlights and back again. In the range were Sweptline pickups, Sweptline Power Wagons and crew-cab Power Wagons. The company also offered a number of derivatives including a fully enclosed Power Wagon, known as the Town Wagon, in 1962.

The same decade did not get off to such a good start for Studebaker. The last years of the 1950s had been difficult ones for the company, until they introduced the Lark passenger car that sold well and improved the financial situation of the company considerably. There were no Lark-type pickup trucks but there were Lark panel vans and the Lark's name later appeared on the Studebaker Champ pickups. The Champ went on sale in 1960 in both 4x2 and 4x4 forms, as did the Transtar alongside which the Champ was manufactured and sold. Studebaker trucks were manufactured only until 1963.

International Harvester had made headlines with the 1961 introduction

RIGHT: A new designation scheme assigned 10, 20, or 30 to half, three-quarter and one-ton models. Since 1957, trucks were available from the factory as four-wheel drive, and the new class scheme would make this known. A C (conventional) in front of the series number as this C10 indicates two-wheel rear drive, while a K denotes four-wheel drive

and so the 1960 trucks went forward into 1961 completely unchanged with some styling changes being§ made for 1962. The hood was lowered and rounded off eliminating the vents in the leading edge and a single long vent was positioned between the parking lights. Other minor changes included a change of hub caps and redesigned badges. This redesign also carried GMC's trucks on through the 1963 model year.

The 1960s were important years for Dodge who built a comprehensive line of pickups. The redesigned Dodge cabs were lower and wider than those that had gone before and mounted on new chassis with different wheelbases. Future revisions were minimal and, for example, included a switch from single

LEFT: In 1960-62, C trucks were available in smooth 'Fleetside' (pictured) or fendered 'Stepside' versions. Half-ton models were the C10 in both long-bed and short-bed truck forms

of the Scout, one of the first 'sport utilities', although that particular term had not yet been coined. It was a boxy, small pickup with rounded corners and a truck cab designed to seat three. The tailgate hinged downwards and the cab roof was removable. The grille was rectangular and single circular headlights were positioned at either side. The Scout was available in both two and four-wheel-drive versions, rated as a quarter-ton and known as the Model 80. It was powered by an in-line four-cylinder engine and constructed around a 100inch wheelbase. The Scout proved to be a success and in excess of 28,000 were sold in 1961. The IHC C-series pickups were a comprehensive range and upgraded versions of the earlier B-series models. The C-100/C-102 models were half-ton trucks based on a 119inch wheelbase, C-110/C-112 trucks were three-quarter-ton trucks on a variety of wheelbases, C-120/C-122 were one-tonners also based on various wheelbases as were the C-130/C-132 models. Both the Model 80 Scout and the C-series of pickups continued for 1962 with only minimal changes. Roll up windows were an option on the Scout and the doors were removable for off-road use and the windshield hinged down flat. There were similar models of the Scout for 1963 and 1964 although the pickup line was restyled. >>

LEFT: A lowered custom 1962 Chevrolet C10 Stepside with the currently popular pátina finish

BELOW LEFT AND BELOW RIGHT: Dodge Trucks saw a complete re-engineering in both style and performance for 1961. Codenamed the R pickup, the new truck featured upgraded styling, more powerful standard engines, higher load capacities and improved interior comfort. The 1961 Sweptline pickups featured a long bodyline that extended from front to rear

RIGHT: The front end of the '61 Dodge Truck looked tough and stylish with four headlights, a full width hood and slotted aluminium grille. The 1961 Dodge Truck blended style, function and comfort. The new cabs were called, 'Drivemasters' and included a huge wraparound front windshield

RIGHT AND MIDDLE: In 1962 a completely new 'J' line of Jeep Gladiator trucks was introduced for the 1963 model year. The Gladiator full-size pickup trucks shared the same platform, front-end styling, and powertrain as the Wagoneer. The Gladiator was available in either 120inch (J-200) or 126in (J-300) wheelbase form. Available configurations included the Thriftside (narrow box), Townside (wide box), Chassis or Cab, stake bed, wrecker and chassis-mounted campers with an extended wheelbase

BELOW: The Studebaker Champ was a light-duty pickup truck produced by the Studebaker Corporation from 1960-1964. The company's financial position forced the use of a number of existing components. The chassis of the Champ was basically the same as that on Studebaker's previous E-series trucks but the cab was redesigned to compete with the Ford Ranchero and Chevrolet El Camino. Two widths of cargo boxes were offered

utility vehicles; a 1965 survey of IHC Scout buyers showed that around 75% of Scouts were purchased for non-business use and 82% of them were purchased in 4x4 form. Also growing rapidly during the mid-1960s was the US commitment to South Vietnam. In March 1965, two battalion landing teams of the US Marine Corps were the first ground combat troops committed to Vietnam and by 1966 the Vietnam War had cost America $5.8 billion.

The Dodge Deora

In 1965 looking further towards the future Chevrolet built another futuristic

The recreational user pickup market was growing rapidly during the mid-1960s and brought changes to the ranges offered by the likes of Chevrolet who, in 1965, introduced a 325cid V8-powered long box model suitable demountable camper fitment. Also introduced was a camper special that had beefed up power train and chassis components. IHC were also aware of this growing recreational market for

concept truck, the Turbo Titan III, with a gas turbine engine for power. It was displayed at auto shows and two years later Dodge displayed their concept truck, the Deora. The Dodge Deora was fitted with an internal combustion engine but offered car-like comfort in a pickup. It was a gold-painted 1965 Dodge A100 pickup truck customised by Mike and Larry Alexander in Detroit to be displayed at the 1967 Detroit Autorama. The Alexander brothers commissioned the design from Harry Bentley Bradley an American car designer, best known for his work with Mattel Hot Wheels and General Motors. The A100 was chopped,

sectioned and channelled to create a fully functional, futuristic-looking machine. The 170cid slant-six engine and three-speed manual transmission were moved back 15inches taking it out of the cab and into the load bed where it was covered by a hard tonneau. Access to the truck was achieved by lifting up the windshield that was made from the back hatch of a 1960 Ford station wagon and swivelling the lower gate and entering through the front. Chrysler subsequently leased the Deora for two years to display with its other factory concept cars and a model version of the Deora was part of the first Hot Wheels model line in 1968.

In many ways these vehicles anticipated the sport-utility market by at least 15 years. Despite Chevrolet's use of a gas turbine engine in their concept machine their internal combustion engines had plenty of miles left in them and in 1965 registrations of their trucks exceeded the 500,000 level. It was a boom time for America's number one truck maker and a year later they sold its 10 millionth pickup. The company's trucks were redesigned for 1967 and optional interior packages including the CS and CST were offered. Chevrolet felt that this redesign was, 'the most significant cab and sheet-metal styling change' in its history and certainly the trucks acquired a much more 'modern' appearance. They appeared longer and lower and much closer to the styling of cars of the time. This was as a result of the trend towards pickups for personal transportation and leisure vehicles as well as working vehicles. The trucks were redesigned to slant inwards above the waistline and to incorporate a swage line that defined the wheel wells and body sides. The area of glass in the windshield and side windows was increased and the elongated appearance was reflected in the grille that featured two long narrow rectangular panels. The new C-10 was offered on two wheelbases in both Fleetside and Stepside forms and as either a 4x2 truck or a 4x4. The only noticeable change

for 1968 was the inclusion of additional chrome trim and badges to the trucks.

Hot on the heels of this redesign came Chevrolet's first full size 4x4, the Blazer in 1969. The suspension arrangement on the Blazer was to use tapered single leaf springs at the front and multi leaf springs at the rear. The 4x4 Blazer base model was powered by an in-line six-cylinder engine although V8s were optional as were manual or automatic transmissions, power steering, power brakes and a removable fibreglass hardtop. The colours, exterior trim, interior trim and general equipment »

For 1964, the Chevrolet C series cab underwent a major update. While sharing the roof and floor structure, the windshield and A-pillar were redesigned, eliminating the intrusive dogleg and the redesign also included an update of the dashboard and door panels. This C10 Fleetside is powered by the optional 283ci (4.6l) Chevrolet small-block V8 engine

were not dissimilar to that used on the K-10 4x4 models of pickup.

Sports Utility Vehicles

The IHC Scout was partially redesigned and upgraded for 1965, a new grille, new hood emblems and a permanently fixed windshield were among these upgrades. The windshield wipers, pedals and numerous interior details were also improved. The Scout was still available in both 4x2 and 4x4 form, although 82% of the Scouts sold in 1965 were 4x4 models. The company also found that half of Scout buyers had never bought an International before and that trade-ins against Scouts included a large proportion of both sports cars and station wagons. These findings influenced IHC who marketed Scouts with increasingly luxurious

RIGHT: The 1964 C series range included stepside pickup trucks (pictured), fleet side pickups, chassis-cab trucks, and medium/heavy commercial versions

interiors and for 1966 offered in-line six-cylinder engines and, later in the same year, V8 options.

In 1966 the Ford Bronco appeared in three styles, roadster pickup, sport utility pickup and wagon intended to compete for sales with both the Jeep and International Harvester's Scout. The Bronco was the first light utility 4x4 built by Ford since its wartime production of the GPW Jeep. While the Ford Bronco was grabbing the headlines, changes were made to the company's truck range that included front disc brakes and optional air conditioning. Also new for 1966 was the change of base vehicle for the Ranchero, instead of using the Falcon platform it was now based on the Fairlane. The F-100 truck was restyled for 1967 but remained available as styleside, flareside, chassis-cab and platform and stake models as well as two longer wheelbase models. The

for 1968 and 1969 were minimal although larger displacement V8s were available.

By 1967, in excess of 800,000 American businesses depended on automobile use and more than 13 million people were employed in businesses that utilised buses and trucks. In the same year more than $13 billion worth of auto parts were produced for the auto industry by other industries and, reflecting the growth in recreational use of light trucks, more than 625,000 mobile homes and campers were produced. The number of mobile homes, travel trailers and truck campers produced the following year exceeded an estimated 818,000. »

ABOVE: A 1964 Chevrolet C series truck with more recent updates that suggest it is still being used commercial. The windscreen sticker refers to its retro-fitted 427ci Chevrolet V8 engine

LEFT AND BELOW: The styling of these early sixties C series trucks endears them to new owners who preserve their patina

F-250 remained as the three-quarter-ton variant available with as many body types and two crew-cabs, namely a styleside and a chassis cab. The one-ton F-350 was offered as a flareside pickup and a chassis/cab but also in two wheelbases with platform and stake bed bodies. There were also long wheelbase F-350 crew cabs in styleside and chassis/cab variants.

The GMC trucks for 1967 were completely redesigned in both styling and engineering features. A number of safety features including seatbelts, four-way flashing hazard lights and a dual braking system were included as standard. The overall shape was more slab sided but sharp radii had been eliminated in favour of rounded edges giving a modern look to the trucks, something that was complemented by the simple radiator grille and dual headlamps. Following this major redesign, the changes

The Travelall by International IH

RIGHT: The Travelall was a line of vehicles manufactured by International Harvester. This, the third-generation version, was produced from 1961 to 1968. It was derived from the International light truck line and was a truck-based station wagon

ABOVE RIGHT: For 1964 and 1965, Dodge offered the Custom Sports Special pickup (pictured) with a $1,300 High Performance pack, and narrow stripes down its centre. This offered a 426ci Wedge engine, with power steering, a HD instrument cluster and tachometer, a LoadFlite automatic, rear axle struts, and dual exhausts. It is believed that fewer than 50 were built

RIGHT: In 1964 Dodge introduced the A100 van on a 90inch wheelbase with its Slant Six engine for power. The 174hp 273ci was fitted the next year, when all Dodge trucks switched to a five-year, 50,000-mile warranty

BELOW RIGHT: By 1965 the Jeep Gladiator full-size pickup trucks based on the large Jeep Wagoneer platform, was part way through its production run that ran from 1962-1988. This design is noteworthy for remaining in production for more than 26 years on a single automobile platform

The war still raged in Vietnam and in 1967 the US Army was consuming 850,000 tons of supplies and 80 million gallons of gasoline monthly. At the end of January 1968, the Viet Cong launched the Tet Offensive against Saigon, Hue and other South Vietnamese cities and places such as Khe Sanh and Da Nang became committed to the pages of the history books.

In 1969 the USA spent $28.8 billion fighting the Vietnam War with Chevrolet introducing the Blazer, a full size 4x4, ahead of a similar vehicle from Ford. The Ford Bronco and Ranchero models continued through 1968, 1969 and into the seventies in similar configurations although subsequently the body styles of the Ranchero would be redesigned several times in keeping with the passenger car-like styling. Four-wheel-drive transmissions were available as an extra cost option. In 1968 for example the 4x4 system added an extra $645 to the cost of both the F-100 and F-250 models. In that year the production of the entire range that had been introduced in the autumn of 1967 was a fraction fewer than 415,000 vehicles. For 1967 the IHC Scout was marketed with three different interior and exterior trim levels, Utility, Custom and Sportop. The utility models featured bench seats and painted bumpers. The Custom models featured a number of interior comforts including bucket seats, armrests, sun visors, vinyl trim as well as chromed bumpers and hubcaps. The 'Sportop' featured a slanted back roof hence its name, and inside had bucket seats and other luxury trims as well as chrome mouldings and trims in addition to the bumpers. Alongside these sport utilities, production of pickup trucks and crew cab trucks continued in both two and four-wheel-drive form. Little was changed for 1968 but the company offered limited edition Scout models for the 1969-70 sales season. The Scout Aristocrat included such features as two-tone paint and chrome custom wheels. IHC's line of conventional pickup trucks was redesigned for 1969 and given a wide flat hood and slab-sided fenders, a design which was reminiscent of the continuing Scout models that were still successful despite the introduction of competing vehicles by the rival manufacturers.

The last year of the 1960s was the year that saw men, Neil Armstrong and Buzz Aldrin, on the moon as the USA won the space race. It had started in 1961 when the USSR made Cosmonaut Yuri Gagarin the first man in space. Overshadowing this was something else that the USA was embroiled in but seemingly could not win, the Vietnam War. In May 1969 units of the US Army and South Vietnamese forces attempted to take Hill 937, aka Hamburger Hill, in the A Shua Valley east of the Laotian border. It turned into one of the

LEFT: **In October 1964, the 1965 F-Series introduced an all-new frame, which would be used until 1979. The body itself remained largely unchanged, but on 1965 and 1966 models the turn signals are above the headlights**

bloodiest battles of the Vietnam War and provoked heavy criticism in the US as the hill had little strategic value.

Elsewhere the counter culture was mobilising; Easy Rider released by Columbia Pictures on 14 July 1969, was a road trip drama written by Peter Fonda, Dennis Hopper, and Terry Southern. Fonda and Hopper, as Wyatt and Billy, play two bikers who travel through the American Southwest and South, carrying the proceeds from a cocaine deal. The success of Easy Rider was heralded as a landmark counterculture film that explored the societal landscape, issues, and tensions towards adolescents in the United States during the 1960s. A month »

LEFT AND BELOW: **Replacing the rudimentary straight-axle in the front was all-new independent 'Twin I-Beam' suspension with coil springs on two-wheel-drive trucks. 1965 and 1966 F-Series trucks are distinguished with a 'Twin I-Beam' emblem on the front fender**

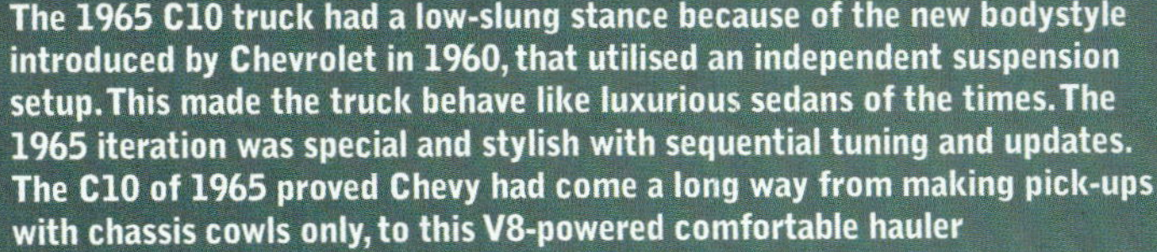

The 1965 C10 truck had a low-slung stance because of the new bodystyle introduced by Chevrolet in 1960, that utilised an independent suspension setup. This made the truck behave like luxurious sedans of the times. The 1965 iteration was special and stylish with sequential tuning and updates. The C10 of 1965 proved Chevy had come a long way from making pick-ups with chassis cowls only, to this V8-powered comfortable hauler

Through the 1960s Chevrolet and GMC trucks were marketed as one and the same. Regardless of what brand you bought, the C10 or G1000 (pictured) was considered a working man's vehicle and its styling now endears it to truck fans

A 1966 half-ton F-100 styleside pickup fitted with a wooden push bumper being used to push Conrad 'Connie' Kalitta dragster, The Bounty Hunter 'fueller', to or from the pits at a race meeting

The Ford Bronco debuted in 1966 and had been developed as a compact off-road vehicle using its own chassis intended to compete for sales against the Jeep CJ-5 and International Harvester Scout

ABOVE: The introduction of 1967 GMC pickup trucks saw all new styling with new sheet-metal extending from a longer nose to lower overall height and a reduced box-to-cab gap. In an upgrade from exposed latches and chains normally found on trucks' tailgates saw the new trucks feature concealed tailgate latches and supports with a centre-mounted latch handle to facilitate one-handed operation

BELOW: Dubbed the 'Action Line, the second-generation C-Series of 1967 added comfort and convenience features to what had previously been a line of work trucks. The design incorporated a simple body side with strong shoulders that taper toward the rear, an integrated fender and hood and a simple grille to achieve a clean appearance. To satisfy customers' power needs, the 1967 C -Series offered a choice of six-cylinder as well as small and big block V8 engines

The M-715 series 1 1/4-ton military Jeep vehicle was designed to replace the Dodge M37 series of three-quarter-ton vehicles that had been in military service since 1951. The M-715 was an adaptation of the Gladiator pickup truck, becoming the first military tactical vehicle built primarily from civilian components. The front grille fenders, hood, doors and cab were stamped from Gladiator dies, with modifications to the upper part of the cab and doors as well as the fender cut-outs while the cargo box was an entirely military design

As this Ford promotional postcard shows, by the late-sixties pick-ups were being marketed as being suitable for recreational purposes as well as commercial

ABOVE AND RIGHT: The Dodge Deora is a 1965 A100 pickup truck that was heavily modified by brothers Mike and Larry Alexander to design by Harry Bentley Bradley, who later works for Hot Wheels, in Detroit, Michigan, for the 1967 Detroit Autorama show. After winning numerous awards, it became the prototype for a Hot Wheels car, and was reproduced as a plastic model kit. It was sold in an auction in 2009 for US$324,500.

The 1966 Ford Ranchero used Falcon front sheet-metal, trim, and interior accents on a modified station wagon platform although Rancheros made late in the '66 model year had the same front clip as the Ford Fairlane

later the Woodstock Music and Art Fair, generally referred to as Woodstock, was a music festival held in Bethel, New York, 40 miles southwest of the town of Woodstock. The festival has become widely regarded as a pivotal moment in popular music history as well as a defining event for the counterculture generation against the backdrop of the unpopular Vietnam War.

That war became noted, amongst other things, as the first helicopter war in history and it is not stretching credibility too far to suggest that the Bell HU-1 'Huey' synonymous with images of the war was the pickup truck of the unfriendly skies. Combat troops, casualties and cases of supplies, the Huey trucked them all and more. During the conflict 4865 US helicopters of all types were shot down.★

DODGE NEWS PHOTO

FROM SNUB NOSED WORKHORSE to showroom beauty: Before and after photos above illustrate the transformation of a standard Dodge A-100 compact pickup truck to the Dodge Deora customized by the Alexander Brothers of Detroit. Original unit was 14 feet, 3 inches long, 6 1/2 feet high. Deora (Spanish for Golden) is nearly 16 feet in length and is 4 feet, 9 inches high. Unique features include retractable front window, center-hinged front door, and swing-away steering wheel to allow driver entrance from frontal area. Another feature is a hidden tail light system.

From: Dodge Public Relations, P. O. Box 1259, Detroit, Michigan 48231
(67-837CPBP)

ABOVE LEFT AND ABOVE RIGHT: International's redesigned C-Series trucks of 1961 were far more evolutionary than revolutionary; however, the models were seen as a new design. Annual model year changes weren't the norm during this time for International Harvester, which tended to focus on integrating minor running changes as needed, with specific changes oriented towards the end of the calendar year. The 1966 run became the A-Series, from the 1000A to the 1300A. Similarly, 1967 trucks were renamed the B-Series, an example is this 1967 1100B half-ton (The numbers being displayed in the load bed mark the brand's 60th anniversary in 1967), with the 1968 model year trucks returning to the C-Series designation of the 1000C through 1300C models

LEFT: For 1968, Dodge installed more V-8 engines than six-cylinders in its light trucks, as buyers demanded similar performance that they were accustomed to in cars. The 1968 model trucks had a new grille that fully surrounded the headlamps while the round front marker lamps were gone, replaced by vertical, rectangular lamps

ABOVE LEFT AND ABOVE RIGHT: Building on the successful first generation of C series pickup, Chevrolet launched a revised version in 1967. Coil springs remained at all four corners beneath the restyled C10, but crisp, clean lines appeared on the outside. Both Stepside and Fleetside (pictured) availability carried over from 1966, and revised grilles were installed new model-year trucks through 1972

LEFT: The Truck, Utility, quarter-ton, 4×4, M151 was the successor to the Korean War M38 and M38A1 Jeeps and served in the Vietnam War. The M151 had an integrated body design which offered a little more space than prior jeeps, and featured all-around independent suspension with coil springs. In various guises it was produced from 1959 through 1982, the M151A1 of 1964 was the second version. The third version was the M151A2 of 1968 (pictured in Berlin) with significantly revised rear suspension that greatly improved safety

1970s

Economic struggle and technological innovation

In Vietnam, on 5 September 1970, Operation Jefferson Glenn began. It was carried out by troops of the 101st Airborne Division (Airmobile) and infantry units of the South Vietnamese Army against 'Charlie' in Vietnam's Thua Thien Province. The operation was to be the last major military operation in Vietnam in which US ground troops would participate. Over the years there have been suggestions that the design of American automobiles reflects how good the country is feeling about itself on an almost year-by-year basis. It may be an apocryphal indicator of the nation's outlook but when viewed in the most general terms it does appear to have some credibility. Truck and car styling was flamboyant in the euphoric postwar years but decidedly lacklustre by the uncertain years of the early 1970s. The decade would see President Richard M. Nixon scaling down, and subsequently ending, US

involvement in the Vietnam War faced with ever increasing opposition to the war at home.

At the time the US automakers were also operating numerous assembly plants around the world including 50 in South America, 60 in Europe, 17 in Africa, 40 in Asia and 27 in Oceania. Although these figures would have shifted significantly by 1973 there was concern about the volume of US domestic auto production when compared to the number of imported vehicles. In 1970 imported vehicles numbered more than 2,000,000 while domestic factories produced in the region of 8,200,000 vehicles. This latter figure accounted for 15.9% of America's steel production as well as 41.2% of iron and 8.2% of aluminium. »

ABOVE AND BELOW: The standard truck bed style tends to be the slab-sided type where the wheel well arches are contained within the bed. Another style of truck bed features visible rounded fenders outside of the truck bed. This reduces the carrying capacity of the truck but, as the name implies, it also adds a step to the forward area of the fender where the bed meets the cab

Chevrolet's Blazer was the first of the full-size, big-engined vehicles based on the idea of a shortened 4x4 pickup chassis. The Blazer first appeared during the 1969 model year in both six and eight-cylinder engine types and was designed to be assembled from existing and proven Chevrolet and GMC light truck components that would ensure it quickly gained market place acceptance. In 1970 Chevrolet's sales were adversely affected by a UAW strike against GMC that lasted 58 days and reduced the American Gross National Product (GNP) by $9 billion. The highest specification Chevy Blazer until 1973 was the CST – Custom Sport Truck – with the Cheyenne Specification package being introduced in 1973, while a roll bar became standard in 1975. All the 4x4 models were leaf sprung front and rear. Two-wheel-drive Blazers were produced from 1970 onwards but proved less popular than the 4x4 models.

GMC put a new product, the GMC Jimmy, on the market in 1970 in order to reap some benefit from the growing recreational vehicle market. Much of its styling was taken from the GMC pickup truck range and it was virtually identical to the Chevrolet Blazer except for some trim parts. The Jimmy was available in both two and four-wheel-drive configurations with a removable hardtop over the rear load bed and front seats. It was designated C1550 and K1550, the prefix varied according to the type of transmission, C indicated 4x2 models while K was 4x4. For the first years of the 1970s the conventional GMC trucks continued to receive only minor upgrades for each year but they, along with the Jimmy, were restyled for 1973.

The introduction of the IHC Scout II came in 1971 and production started alongside that of the Scout and the company's conventional light truck

RIGHT: Chevy uses the term 'Fleetside,' while other brands have their own terminology including 'Townside' for Jeep, 'Sweptline' for Dodge, and 'Wideside' for GMC. However, Fleetside seems to be the most popular term used across the brands for this Chevy's style of truck bed

cylinder engine with a V8 available as an option. The Bronco was otherwise basic and options such as power steering and automatic transmissions were not available until 1973. The Bronco lasted in almost its original guise until 1977 when it was replaced by the upsized Bronco based on the Ford F-150 pickup chassis and closer in concept to the Chevy Blazer.

Apollo 15 put wheels on the moon in 1971 when the astronauts James Irwin and David Scott drove the Boeing-constructed Lunar Roving Vehicle (LRV) several miles on the moon's surface during their mission. Closer to home the trend towards the »

range. The new Scout, introduced in the spring, had been redesigned and now incorporated power brakes, power steering, air conditioning, automatic transmission and a V8 engine. The body was longer and lower than that of the previous models and sales exceeded 30,000 in the first year of production. For 1972 the Scout was discontinued while the Scout II continued upgraded only in minor details such as changes to the radiator grille. The front end of the Scout II was redesigned again for 1973, as was that fitted to the IHC range of trucks. At this time IHC was America's fifth largest truck maker behind Chevrolet, Ford, Dodge and GMC in that order.

From its 1966 introduction, the Ford Bronco was a trendsetter in the four-wheel-drive and sport utility sector of the truck market and the first truly mass-marketed 4x4 in the USA. It featured an innovative coil spring suspension system and an in-line six-

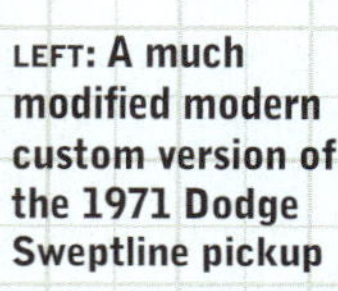

ABOVE: Another modern custom is this 1971 Chevrolet C10 pickup that underwent an extensive restoration and was rebuilt with numerous new components. Under the hood sits an LS3 crate motor with 430 horsepower, a four-speed 4L65-E automatic, Ridetech air suspension, a Be Cool cooling system and custom body panels from Goodmark Industries

RIGHT: As usual the GMC trucks used the same sheet-metal as the Chevrolet models but were named differently. While GMC also used the C (two-wheel-drive) and K (four-wheel-drive) model designators, they differed from Chevrolet in that they used four-digit numbers for the weight range. As such, 1971 half-tons were 1500s, three-quarter-tons were 2500s, and one-tons were 3500. Therefore, a half-ton two-wheel drive GMC was a C1500

recreational use of trucks was growing ever stronger. In 1972 the popularity of mobile homes, camper trailers, truck campers, travel trailers and truck covers was such that a rise in pickup sales was recorded as part of the surge in recreational vehicle (RV) sales. Pickups were used to haul trailers and carry camper bodies. At the time it was noted that the average RV family spent 10% of its time using the vehicle and consisted of four persons headed by a whitecollar worker. This was in stark contrast to the pickup's distinctly bluecollar roots and, of course, continuing industrial and agricultural use.

In 1972 the method of construction used for the car-styled Ford Ranchero was changed. To make it bigger and stronger it now featured a separate chassis and body as opposed to the previous car-like monocoque construction. A sports version was known as the Ranchero GT Sedan-Pickup and the Squire variant featured imitation wood panels along the sides and a number of other trim detail upgrades. The base models were powered by an in-line six while the base GT models featured a V8. There were numerous V8 options that included 302, 351, 400, 429 cubic inch displacement engines as well as both manual and automatic transmissions. That year's styling changes to the conventional F-100 and F-250 truck models were considerably more limited and restricted to things such as a redesigned grille and interior detail upgrades.

For 1973 the F-100 and F-250 were changed considerably more than

LEFT: Production of the fifth generation of the Ford F-Series came to an end in 1972. Three trim levels were available during the production of the fifth generation F-Series, though the names were changed in 1970.

BELOW: The base trim became the 'Custom' and the 'Custom Cab' became the 'Sport Custom' (pictured) joining 'Ranger' as optional levels of equipment and trim in 1970 for 1971 model year trucks

the Ranchero models. The hood was redesigned with a flatter face and the cab was longer to provide behind-the-seats storage, with the side accent on the body changing from raised to indented. Chassis-cab, flareside and styleside variants were offered. Production of the first two models totalled less than 6,000 while production of styleside models exceeded 457,000. The F-250 models were restyled in a similar way and proportions of the production run were also similar. The total production of all three F-250 variants was approximately 198,000 vehicles. In the case of the one-ton F-350 models though the largest production was the 42,000 chassis-cab »

ABOVE LEFT AND ABOVE RIGHT: Mickey Thompson (1928-1988) was an American hot rodder who pursued land speed records in his late 20s and early 30s. He achieved international fame in 1960, when he became the first American to break the 400mph barrier, driving his Challenger 1 to a one-way top speed of 406.60 mph at the Bonneville Salt Flats. Thompson then turned to track and drag racing and entered cars at the Indianapolis 500. He went into the performance aftermarket business in the early 1960s and then, in 1963, he manufactured Mickey Thompson Performance Tires for racing. Thompson founded SCORE International in 1973, a sanctioning body to oversee off-road racing across North America. His first off-road race truck was a 1972 Chevy C10 however it couldn't take the punishment that he put it through so he built a larger 1973 Chevy C20 for the next season. In 1988, Thompson and his wife Trudy were murdered at their home in California by a former business partner

ABOVE: The third generation of the C and K series trucks that were manufactured by General Motors replaced this second-generation model for the 1973-1991 model years. This is the fleetside, the most common type of truck bed and the name chosen by Chevy and GMC, as well as Dodge and others

RIGHT: The second generation of GMC Jimmy was introduced for the 1973 model year. It was an upmarket version of the Chevrolet K5 Blazer, and was available with in-line six and V8 engines and even a diesel option. Until 1975, the Jimmy was offered with a full removable hardtop, but from 1976 onward, a half-cab configuration was used

models and a total of only 26,600 of all the other variants including stylesides, chassis-cowl, platforms, parcel vans and P-400 models. This reflects the F-350's suitability for the installation of specialist rear bodies for agricultural and industrial uses.

On 27 January 1973, the signing of the Peace Accords in Paris, brought an end to the Vietnam War. It had been the longest war in American history and the nation had suffered in excess of 58,000 killed or missing in action. The war had significant socio-economic effects that included the resignation of a president, the political turmoil it engendered and the economic problems of the early 1970s.

Light truck sales tapered off during 1973 due to the 'gas crisis' engendered by the Arab oil embargo. Although this precipitated the trend towards smaller more economic trucks in this period, Chevrolet introduced a truck powered by the 454cid V8 and sold its 15 millionth truck. Despite this, during this period, Ford regained the lead in sales from Chevrolet. The biggest threat to the Ford company however was no longer from Chevrolet but from imported compact trucks. In this year Japanese Datsun (later Nissan) and Toyota were selling their Li'l Hustler and Hilux trucks respectively. The latter truck was

ABOVE LEFT AND ABOVE RIGHT: The second-generation Ford Econoline van was launched in January 1968 for model year 1969. This second-generation Econoline became a heavier-duty vehicle, sharing many of its underpinnings with the F-Series full-sized pickups and it remained in production until 1974

LEFT: During the 1970s, the GM Medium duty range was completely redesigned based on the recently introduced all-new design of full-size pickups. Numerous models were offered including the C-50, C-60, C-65 and the 5000, 6000 (pictured) and 6500

based around a 101.6inch wheelbase and weighed 2,480 pounds. The Hilux was powered by a water-cooled, in-line, four-cylinder overhead camshaft engine that displaced 120cid and produced 97 bhp @ 5500 rpm. These compact imports sold well because of their low price meaning both Ford and Chevrolet needed to compete.

Ford sourced a Mazda truck from Toyo Kogyo of Japan, they described it as the Courier and badged it as a Ford. The Courier was built to Ford's specifications and included rubber mounts between the cab and the chassis frame. It was powered by an in-line, four-cylinder, water-cooled, 74bhp engine connected to a four-speed stick shift transmission. The Courier had

BELOW: Ford's mid-1970s medium duty truck was the fifth-generation F-Series that had been introduced for the 1967 model year, with Ford diverging the design of its light-duty and medium-duty F-Series. To streamline production costs, medium-duty trucks retained the cab and hood of light-duty trucks. A solid front axle was installed with redesigned front fenders to accommodate the wider track and larger wheels

RIGHT: The sixth generation of the Ford F-Series, often referred to as the 'dentside' Ford by enthusiasts, was a line of pickup trucks and medium-duty commercial trucks that were produced by Ford Motor Company from the 1973-1979 model years. It included the all-new Ford F-150 (pictured), a heavy-duty half ton companion to the popular F-100. This meant that Ford's pickup truck line now comprised of four models; F-100, F-150, F-250 and the big F-350

RIGHT: Jeep dropped the Gladiator name in 1971, after which the line was known simply as the Jeep pickup designated as J2000 and J4000 models, until 1973, then as J10 and J20 models (pictured) designating payload capacity, from 1974 to 1988. The AMC 258ci in-line six engine was introduced in 1972 and offered until 1988. Larger brakes were fitted as standard and the turning radius reduced

RIGHT: In 1976, Jeep's popular Honcho model appeared and cost $699 more than a standard custom level J-10 shortbed. It was the truck equivalent of the WIDE-TRACK CHEROKEE CHIEF AND INCLUDED TWO VERSIONS: the step-bed Sportside and the Townside. It featured gold striping on the bedside, fenders and tailgate, wide 8x15 spoked wheels and off-road tires, Levi's denim interior and a sport steering wheel

a payload of 1400 pounds and a load bed larger than its competitors of the time. In 1972, Isuzu of Japan supplied its mini-pickups to Chevrolet, they were badged as Chevy LUVs. The LUV designation was an acronym for Light Utility Vehicle but also had the ring of 1970s' slang to it. The LUV sold well and more than 21,000 were sold in the period between March and December 1972.

Chevrolet offered its half and three-quarter-ton trucks with a 4x4 option from 1973, the same year as the 15 millionth truck was made by the company. Interior trim was now offered as the Custom, Custom Deluxe, Cheyenne and Cheyenne Super range.

LEFT: A step-side Honcho during an off-road competition. The J-10 J-Series pickup truck line included the Honcho, Golden Eagle and 10-4 trim packages. All shared the same body design as the Wagoneer and Cherokee from the cab forward, and were offered with traditional slab-sided or step-side bodies. The 10-4 trim package was produced from 1974-1983

Sales topped the 920,000 mark and despite the gas crisis the 454cid engine was greeted with immediate acclaim. The next year the interior packages were to be renamed Silverado and Scottsdale that helped Chevrolet become dominant in the light 4x4 truck market. Chevrolet's full-size pickups were completely redesigned for 1973 and the new design featured squared off wheel arches, sculpted body sides, a roomier cab with more glass area and an egg crate-style radiator grille. Trim levels available included Custom, Custom Deluxe, Cheyenne and Cheyenne Super specifications. For 1974 full time 4x4 was available in the four-wheel-drive models through use of the NP203 transfer case in V8 models. California emissions legislation meant that the in-line six-cylinder engine was not available in that state. For 1975 the 400cid small block V8 was added to the list of optional engines and the NP203 transfer case became standard on all the V8 automatic transmission models. The manual models retained the conventional part time system with locking hubs. In the interior the Custom trim level was deleted making the custom deluxe the base trim.

1974 was the year of the Watergate scandal and President Nixon's resignation as the US Congress moved to impeach him. Gerald R. Ford became the 38th President of the USA. The year was a more auspicious one for the nation's truck makers. Dodge had redesigned its trucks at the beginning of the 1970s to incorporate independent front suspension, lower ▸▸

LEFT AND BELOW: The United States military instituted the Commercial Utility Cargo Vehicle (CUCV) Program to provide cheaper, light utility vehicles to augment purpose-built machines. Dodge supplied mildly militarized civilian trucks in 1976 and 1977. Rather than being purely tactical trucks these, the M880 series of vehicles, was the use of commercial vehicles with minor modifications in non-combat roles. The basic 4x4 vehicle of the series, the M880 pickup, was created from the Dodge three-quarter-ton W200 pickup. A 4x2 version was based on the D200 chassis and designated the M890. A folding set of steel bows was available to support a cargo cover over the standard civilian bed

The civilian Dodge D-series pickups included the 1978 Dodge Adventurer club cab sweptline W200 (pictured). Dodge had pioneered the extended-cab pickup with its introduction of the club cab with the 1973 models. Available with either a 78inch or 96inch sweptline bed, the club cab was a two-door cab with small rear windows. It had more space behind the seats than the standard cab but was not as long as the four-door crew-cab truck

RIGHT: The PW100 Trailduster was an SUV manufactured by Plymouth with a three-door wagon body on a 106inch wheelbase. Various engines were offered for this full-time 4x4 with a two-speed transfer case and a choice of manual three and four-speed or automatic gearboxes

and wider cabs and a new interior. The list of available options was increased to include components including electronic ignitions and an industry-first was the 'club-cab', an extended cab model. The grille was redesigned for 1974 and the Ramcharger, a 4x4 sport utility, was launched. Innovation continued through the 1970s, with full time 4x4 systems, a 4x2 Ramcharger and a dual rear wheel arrangement option for one-ton pickups of 1975 and 1976 all being offered.

At Ford production of both the Ford Bronco and Ranchero continued with only minor changes being made. The styling of the F-100, F-250 and F-350 remained unchanged but an extended cab model known as the SuperCab, was made available. It was offered in all three payloads and almost 30,000 were produced in the first year. Ford production of its 1974 range introduced on 1 September 1973 exceeded the one million mark for the calendar year. This surpassed that of Chevrolet and allowed Ford to retain its position at number one. Ford offered 4x4 variants of both the F-100 and F-250 in the same year and followed this with the F-150, a half-ton truck, that became available in 1975. A 4x4 variant of the latter pickup followed in 1976.

The IHC Scout went forward into 1974 unchanged while the pickups were given new designations becoming the 100 and 200 models for the half and three-quarter-ton respectively. The pickups remained in production until 1975 when the line was discontinued, as was the travelall model. Production of light trucks by Plymouth had been stopped on the outbreak of »

RIGHT: The 1978 version of the Chevrolet K5 Blazer, a full-size sport-utility vehicle that was built by General Motors and part of the Chevrolet C/K truck family. For 1976, GM introduced the half-cab design that was less prone to leaks and slightly safer in a roll-over. The second generation K5 models incorporated the rear hatch glass and tailgate into a single unit (pictured), that allowed the glass panel to retract inside of the tailgate

The GMC 1978 Custom Deluxe, two-wheel-drive, stepside version of the third generation of the C/K Series trucks. These were distinguished by the straight-lines, boxy appearance, of the cab and front sheet metal leading to them gaining the nickname of 'square-body' trucks

BELOW LEFT: In 1978, Ford introduced the Ranger F-150 extended cab pickup. It was available with either a short or long bed and was also available with four-wheel-drive (pictured). There were a total of 10,358 extended cab Ranger F-150 trucks made in 1978

BELOW RIGHT: The J20 was offered in half-ton and thee-quarter-ton capacities with five different bodywork options, namely, cab and chassis, chassis-mounted campers with extended wheelbases, stake bed (pictured), wrecker, and load bed. The latter was divided into two types of load bed, Townside and Thriftside - wide and narrow boxes respectively

LEFT AND ABOVE: During the late-seventies, after the 1973 fuel crisis, mini-trucking in compact and imported trucks became popular for recreation. Stepside bed conversions as well as roll bars, custom wheels and custom paint work all became popular. What's more it was a fashion that spread around the world, as these Mazdas in Great Britain display

World War Two and was not resumed until 1974 when the company released the Trail Duster. The Trail Duster was a slab-sided vehicle typical of trucks of the time and available as an open machine with a choice of either a soft top or a fibreglass roof. The 1974 model was available with a 106inch wheelbase and was a 4x4 powered by a V8 with an automatic transmission with a number of shift positions for off-road use. A 4x2 variant of the Trail Duster was introduced in 1975 featuring independent front suspension in place of the driven live axle. The 4x4 model continued as before although minor trim and colour changes were made and a 'sport package' was offered as an extra cost option. This was repeated for 1976.

Production of an unchanged Ford Ranchero continued in 1975 although the Bronco was revised with the fitment of a stronger rear axle >>

RIGHT: Dodge had used the Power Wagon nameplate since the late-forties and decided to boost late-seventies sales with some special badges including the Power Wagon Macho Edition. This was a special edition of the W150 4×4 pickup truck that came with a factory roll bar and a set of 10-15 LT-B tyres fitted to eight-spoke wheels. The Macho Power Wagon trucks all featured special paint. The primary colour was usually bright red or orange a glossy black stripe along the bottom of the body and on the hood

RIGHT: Dodge's 1979 pickups ranged from the basic Dodge D150 working pickup with a choice of wide or narrow boxes - sweptline or utiline respectively - and club cab and single cab variants alongside limited edition models such as the L'il Red Truck

FAR RIGHT: The 1979 Chevy four-wheel-drive trucks, as pickups and Blazers, were part of the longest running line of Chevy trucks, which lasted 14 years from 1973 to 1987. This line of truck started with dramatic changes in 1973 that revised the body, the power plants and the trim packages available. During this era, numerous innovations were introduced and four-wheel drive was made available on all conventional trucks up to one-ton

reflecting its popularity for off-road use. Later in the year it was further upgraded and fitted with disc brakes on the front axle. Exterior styling remained unchanged on Ford's range of pickups and only minor upgrades were made elsewhere. The range continued as it was with only a minor facelift for 1976, the year of America's bicentennial. The long-running Bronco was designated the U-150 in 1978 and redesigned so as to achieve greater commonality parts with those of the F-series trucks and to upgrade its appearance. Sales more than doubled in the following 12 months and took Ford into the eighties along with the further redesigned fleet of F-prefixed trucks. In 1976 a survey in Popular Mechanics magazine found that 53.9% of Ford van buyers used their vehicles for recreation.

In 1977 Gary Gilmore was executed in a Utah State Prison, the first convict to be executed in the USA in ten years, and in the same year Chevrolet saw its sales exceed one million per year. After 60 years of truck manufacture the company had made a total of 21,850,083 trucks. The LUV models had put Chevrolet firmly into the mini-truck market and were to maintain the company's strong position in

this sector until the introduction of the compact Chevrolet S-10 in 1981. The 1977 Chevy LUV was available in two wheelbase lengths, 102.4 and 117.9inches and was, according to the sales brochure for that year, 'tough enough to be a Chevy'. The LUV was powered by a four-cylinder 80bhp engine and according to Environmental Protection Agency (EPA) estimates returned 34 mpg on the highway and 24 mpg in urban use. Numerous options were available including the Mighty Mike decal package, a rear step bumper, an automatic transmission, air conditioning and an AM/FM radio. Interior trim levels included the more luxurious Mikado package with a further option of high back bucket seats in place of the bench seat.

The K30 4x4 one-ton models were added to the full-size Chevrolet line up in 1977 and with them came Bonus Cab and Crew Cab models. The grille was redesigned and power windows were added to the list of available options. The K prefix continued to indicate a Chevrolet 4x4 model and by 1977 it was possible to buy a GMC K3500 crew cab wideside 4x4 pickup, the 4x4 option adding $1248 to the base price. Other variations were available such as the Desert Fox trim option of 1978 that reflected the popularity of off-road desert racing in the USA. Indy Hauler trucks were also built to mark the GMC company's involvement with the Indy 500 when GMC trucks were the official speedway trucks during the famous race. In 1978 the Chevrolet truck »

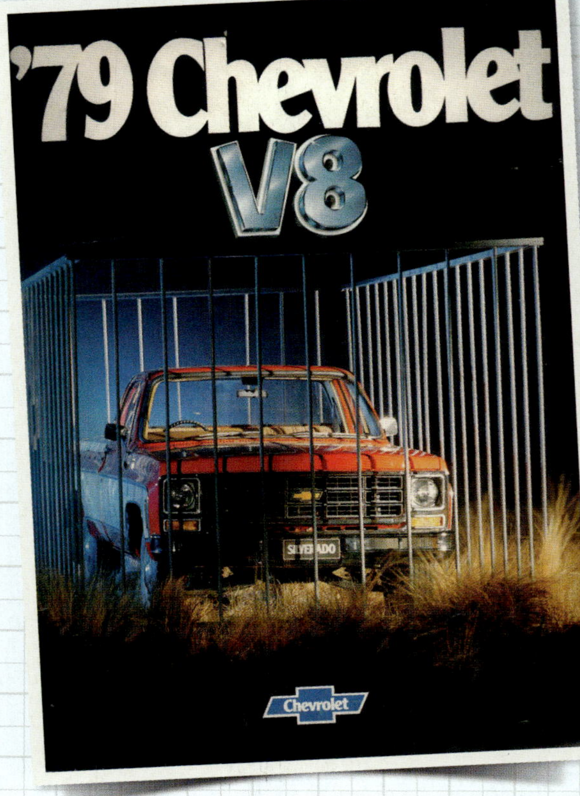

RIGHT: In contrast to the 'square body' nickname, GM called its third generation C/K trucks the 'Rounded Line' models. They were the longest-produced version of the C/K model line, produced for 18 model years until 1991

FAR RIGHT: The International Scout II Terra pickup and Traveler (pictured) were produced from 1976 to 1980. Terras and Travelers had fiberglass tops comprising a half-cab for the Terra or full-top with hatchback-type liftgate on the Traveler. Due to the International Harvester strike of 1979-80, a lack of funds prevented the company from continuing production of the Scout

chassis was slightly redesigned to make space to allow the fitment of catalytic converters, initially required only in California. There were a number of minor styling upgrades for 1979 that included changes to the grille.

In 1977 the front end of the Ford Ranchero was redesigned to incorporate stacked rectangular headlights while production of the other Ford trucks continued in a similar style to before. The variety of options, variations and body types meant that it was possible vehicles such as a F-150 Ranger XLT Flareside 4x4 Pickup. XLT was a trim level and Flareside was Ford's description of their stepside models. The Plymouth Trail Duster vehicles received a minor facelift for 1977 when the grille was redesigned to incorporate horizontal bars and vertical signal lights while the Plymouth badge was shifted from the centre of the grille to the face of the hood. The standard engine was an in-line six-cylinder, although a V8 was also an option. IHC's Scout II remained in production, however, with few changes beyond a slightly different range of optional V8 engines. The production run of the Scout II would last until 1980, after which the company concentrated solely on the heavy truck market. The last years of Scouts saw the models increasingly aimed at the sport utility market, although there were pickups made including the Scout II Terra Compact Sport Pickup.

For 1978, the year Americans bought an estimated four million pickups, the Ford Bronco was completely restyled and now closely resembled the full-size Ford pickups which had also been restyled for this model year. The grille was set higher and featured a rectangular design, the amber lights were set below the headlamps and a

RIGHT AND BELOW: The 1979 GMC Sierra Classic was a model with the third generation of C/K trucks to be produced by General Motors from 1973-1991. The truck often doubled as a personal vehicle for many Americans and Sierra Classic was one of four trim levels offered; Sierra, Sierra Grande, High Sierra, and Sierra Classic. Considered the top trim level, the Sierra Classic trim was offered in wideside or fenderside (pictured) configurations

new bumper was installed. The types of cab and transmission in 4x2 or 4x4 configurations were retained, as were the F-100, F-150, F-250 and F-350 model designations. Things continued in a similar way for 1979 although the trucks were fitted with rectangular headlights. The Plymouth models were left unchanged for 1978 after the 1977 redesign but new options were offered different seats, tinted glass, tilt steering column and a CB radio integrated with the AM/FM stereo. New for 1979 was the Plymouth Arrow, a downsized mini pickup made by Mitsubishi in Japan for Plymouth. The Arrow was powered by an in-line, four-cylinder engine of 122cid displacement. A sport package for the same truck was also offered that included bucket seats, extra dashboard gauges, spoked sport wheels and decals.

Dodge introduced a factory custom truck in 1978 known as the Li'l Red Truck which followed on from its black-painted Warlock model of 1976. Much of the 1970s is remembered as the muscle-car era and, although it was almost over by 1978, the Li'l Red Truck was a fitting swansong as well as being the first muscle-truck. It was based on the D150 truck powered by a 360cid V8, the prototype had W2 cylinder heads and a Holley four-barrel carburettor and would run mid-14s out on the quarter mile strip where muscle-cars decided who was boss. Eventually a slightly lower performance version - it would run mid-fifteens - was offered to the public through Dodge dealers. These were finished in red, trimmed with the 'adventurer' package, wooden bed details and gold decals. The truck

was offered for two consecutive years, in 1978 2,188 were made and in 1979 5,118. The second-year models had dual square headlamps at each side of the grille while the earlier ones had single round lights. The later model featured a catalytic converter as the emission regulations were tightened. Three Li'l Red Trucks ran in the infamous Baja 1000 desert race during 1979 in conjunction with Walker Evans, Dodge's noted off-road racer. Two made it to the finish in La Paz, Mexico while the third suffered a punctured radiator and was forced to retire.

The 1980 range of Chevrolet trucks introduced in the fall of 1979 was as large as ever and included two and four-wheel-drive fleetside and stepside models, as well as two and four-wheel-drive fleetside sport and stepside sport models, two and four-wheel-drive crew cab and bonus cab models, two- and four-wheel -drive chassis-cab models for specialist rear bodies such as wrecker trucks as well as the C-10 diesel pickup and the heavy duty BIG-10 pickup. 'Name the job there's truck here to match' said Chevrolet. Four trim packages were listed Standard Custom Deluxe, Scottsdale, Cheyenne and Silverado. The latter was the most luxurious. The 1980s were just around the corner and times were changing. ★

SUBSCRIBE TODAY
AND SAVE £££S*

SUBSCRIBER BENEFITS

- **EXCLUSIVE** Subscriber offers on the Key Publishing Shop
- **SAVE** over buying individual issues
- **DELIVERED DIRECT** to your door
- **SUBSCRIBER DISCOUNTS** on Key Publishing event tickets
- **BE THE FIRST** to read the latest features

OUR LATEST SUBSCRIPTION OFFERS

BEST VALUE

UK PRINT
1 YEAR
£58.99
Paying by Annual Direct Debit
2 ISSUES FREE!

UK PRINT
6 MONTHS
£32.49
Paying by Credit or Debit Card
SAVE 50p PER ISSUE!

Please quote: **CLR25** when ordering

SCAN THE QR CODE TO ORDER DIRECT FROM OUR SHOP
shop.keypublishing.com/clrsubs

or **call +44 (0)1780 480404** (Lines open 9.00-5.30, Monday-Friday GMT)

Terms and conditions: Quoted rates are for UK subscriptions only, paying one year print or annual direct debit. Standard one-year print subscription prices: UK - £64.99, EU - £71.99, USA - £83.99, ROW - £89.99. All quoted prices subject to change.

CLOSING DATE: December 25th 2025

CLASSIC LAND ROVER

MAY 2025
ISSUE NO 144
£6.29

Key Publishing

*Closing date: 25 Sept. 2025

www.classiclandrover.com

THE WORLD'S BEST-SELLING CLASSIC LAND ROVER MAGAZINE

KEEPING IT IN THE FAMILY

SOMETHING DIFFERENT
How Series III gave me focus

NATIONAL PARK TOUR
Exploring the North York Moors

RIGHT AND FAR RIGHT: The Chevrolet trucks were updated in 1980. While GMC trucks carried over the same grille from 1979, Chevrolet versions received an all-new grille – the first completely new design since 1974. Square headlights made their appearance for the first time on Silverado models. Lower-spec trucks featured a combination of the 1980 grille and the 1979 round headlight surround

THE EIGHTIES
Materialism and Consumerism

With the benefit of hindsight, it seems that the eighties started in a low-key way although the Moscow Olympic games were boycotted by several countries, including the USA, opposed to the USSR's military action in Afghanistan. Ongoing was a presidential race that involved Republican Ronald Reagan and Democrat Jimmy Carter. Disaffected former liberals provided millions of crucial votes for the victory of Reagan, the personable and engaging former governor of California, over the incumbent Democratic president Carter. Soon into his tenure in the White House, Reagan survived an assassination attempt and the Philadelphia Phillies won their first World Series baseball tournament in 98 years.

The arrival of a new Chairman – Lee Iacocca – at Chrysler made the news in automotive circles. As the decade opened Ford advertised the F-100 as the 'first new truck of the eighties' and produced redesigned models including a number of 'custom' paint options with contrasting panels. The model designations remained unchanged so it was, for example, possible to buy a Ford half-ton F-150 Custom flareside 4x4 Pickup. The Ford 4x4 models featured a new front suspension system known as the Twin-Traction Beam »

RIGHT AND FAR RIGHT: GMC's truck range for the 1981 model year included the ongoing half-ton GMC Jimmy and corresponding pickups as well as the Rally STX and Vandura vans in half and three-quarter-ton configurations

RIGHT AND BELOW: Dodge's approach early 1980s to fuel economy came from its alliance with Mitsubishi Motors. The 1981 D50 compact truck came with a 2.0l or 2.6l in-line four-cylinder engine and five-speed manual transmission. In 1982, the four-wheel-drive PowerRam 50 arrived then in 1987, the Mitsubishi Montero-rebadged-Dodge Raider two-door truck was sold, and in 1990 a V6 version was offered

independent suspension. In the same year the Ranchero pickup was dropped from the Ford range.

Recession and Unemployment

Sales of early 1980s models generally dropped because of the poor state of the economy. By early 1982, the United States was experiencing its worst recession since the 1930s. Nine million people were unemployed in November of that year. Businesses closed, families lost their homes and farmers lost their land. Ford continued to sell its compact, Mazda-built, Courier pickups and turned some of their attention to more fuel-efficient vehicles. Styling of the F-Series trucks remained the same, although minor upgrades included removing the word Ford from the front edge of the hood and installing the famous oval blue logo in the centre of the grille. In March 1982 the down-sized Ranger pickup made its debut with styling similar to the F-100. It had become a model in its own right rather than a trim option for an 'Effie' and just a year, later the Bronco II made its debut and sold at two and a half times its previous rate.

The 1979 Chevrolet range of full-size trucks had been the C and K-series pickups, crew cab pickups, fleetside sport pickups and Big Dooleys, a large capacity truck with dual rear wheels. This range continued into 1980 with only minimal changes. A range of vans included the basic van, a sportvan, a nomad van and a caravan and, in addition, there were the suburban and blazer models in two and four wheel drive variants. This range was complemented by the compact Chevy LUV and El Camino trucks. During the 1980s the company adopted a new strategy so stopped manufacturing heavy duty trucks in order to concentrate on the medium and light duty markets. The Silverado models were given rectangular headlights but the major changes came in 1981. GMC made only cosmetic changes to its range of trucks as the company entered the eighties, although the square patterned 'ice-cube tray' radiator grille remained. A styling extra-cost option that showed the direction in which auto-styling was heading, was the dual stacked rectangular headlamps either side of the grille in place of the single circular ones fitted as standard. The half-ton models retained an in-line six-cylinder engine as standard while the other base models had a V8 engine as standard. This programme of minor upgrades continued into the 1981 models. Detail upgrades were made to the transmission of the 4x4 variants, and the front sheet-metal of both Jimmys and pickups was redesigned to make it more aerodynamic and therefore improve fuel efficiency.

New for 1982 from GMC were the S15 model trucks on which work had begun in 1978 as a response to the increasing popularity of the smaller sized imported trucks such as the Chevy LUV, which was really an Isuzu with Chevrolet badges. The S15 was similar in size to the LUV and by 1983 there were 4x4 and extended cab models available. The downsized GMC Jimmy was based around the S15 and featured a tailgate and two doors on a 100.5inch wheelbase and was a four-wheel-drive vehicle. The Chevrolet S-10 of 1982 was a compact that replaced the Chevy LUV and available in two and later four-wheel drive. Dodge shifted production to more aerodynamic pickups and a downsized model, the front-wheel-drive Rampage sport truck.

During 1983 the US Marines suffered more than 200 casualties, killed when their Beirut base was bombed but later in the same month they were the soldiers trusted with the controversial invasion of Grenada to protect its democracy. New for 1984 from Ford was the downsized Bronco II sport utility designed along similar lines to the compact Ranger pickup. The F-100 was discontinued with the F-150 becoming the base model in a range that still included the F-250 and F-350 pickups. By the middle of the decade The Ranger and Bronco II were established in Ford's range of light duty trucks along with the full-size F-150, F-250 and F-350 models. For 1984 the limited-edition GMC Indy Hauler pickup, to commemorate the Indy 500 motor race, was based on an extended cab S15 model. It was one of numerous options offered that year. The full-size GMC truck models continued into the mid-1980s with the same general appearance as had gone before, although the programme of sequential upgrades continued - suspension and engine two areas in which refinements were made. Pickups in both wideside and fenderside variants continued to be manufactured

and as a result of increasing awareness about gas-mileage, diesel options were introduced into the range.

The real news from Ford for 1986 was not so much about its range of pickups but a van when the Aerostar range was introduced. It was to be manufactured by Ford from the 1986 through to the 1997 model years, and was the first minivan produced by Ford. The model line was marketed against the Chevrolet Astro/GMC Safari and the first generations of the Chrysler minivans. Bronco IIs and Ranger pickups remained in the range, as did the F-150, F-250 and F-350 models, selling well given

the disappointing sales earlier in the decade. They had both a record sales year and regained the number one position in US auto sales. The Ford F-Series ran through the 1980s, albeit with considerable changes, but remained as Ford's prime trucks intended to compete with Chevrolet during the first half of the 1990s.

The Farm Crisis

The US economy as a whole was improving, although in January 1987 it was noted that the farming economy was declining generally. This farming crisis completely altered the fabric of rural America »

ABOVE RIGHT: A dealer's promotional postcard to help entice customers to buy the 1984 version of the 1980-1998 generation of F-Series pickups

as farmers confronted an economic crisis more severe than any since the Great Depression. Communities throughout the Midwest and across the nation were devastated, as families were forced from the land, lenders collapsed and businesses on rural main streets closed. It was accepted that the small independent farmer was disappearing and being driven from the land by falling prices. The number of farms was down 9% from 1975 and it was noted that the family farm depression was the worst in 50 years. Such a decline would, of course, have a knock-on effect in rural areas and not least affect the number of pickups sold.

Over the course of the next decade the pickup truck market would shift considerably and sport trucks and sport utilities were to become mainstream America's major auto purchases. The compact Chevrolet S-10 was at the forefront of this trend. By 1991 the S-10 and C-series pickups and their respective Blazer and Suburban sport utility derivatives were as important as each other in the Chevrolet model line-up. The nineties generation of the C- and K-series trucks were available with petrol and diesel engines, short and long load boxes, regular and extended cabs and in three levels of trim, namely Cheyenne, Scottsdale and Silverado. There was a similar degree of choice for purchasers of the S-10 compact pickup with the exception of the diesel -powered variant. The varying trim levels were referred to as Standard and Tahoe and there was an additional Baja off road trim package for 4x4 models. The S-10 Blazer came in two or four door models with choice of 4x2 and 4x4 transmissions and featured an Electronic Fuel Injection (EFI) V6 engine. The trim levels offered were the same as those for the S-10. The full-size Blazer was V8 petrol or diesel powered, with a choice of Scottsdale or Silverado trim and either two- or four-wheel drive. The APV – All Purpose Vehicle – was a new addition to the Chevrolet light truck range, available as the Astro passenger van, the Lumina APV and the Sportvan. A spectacular sport truck from Chevrolet completed the 1991 range, although it was originally introduced in 1989 and was a truck that harked back to the muscle car era of the seventies, the 454 SS. A 454cid V8 powered C1500 fleetside pickup, finished in Onyx Black.

Further from home it took massive American involvement in the 1991 Gulf War on the side of the Coalition Forces to liberate Kuwait from the occupying Iraqi forces and the pickup truck rolled on. ★

After the long wheelbase CJ-6 was phased out in 1975, AMC replaced it with the CJ-8 Scrambler, introduced in 1981 as the 1982 model year truck. It was a small pickup truck, similar to the CJ-7, but was built on a longer 103inch wheelbase with a long rear overhang to increase cargo space. Its components largely paralleled that of the CJ-7, although a V8 was not available in the CJ-8. Known internationally as the CJ-8, the open-cab pickup was available in either soft or hardtop configurations until the Scrambler was replaced by the similarly-sized Jeep Commanche pickup in 1985

ABOVE AND BELOW: For 1982, the Chevrolet C/K models' front grille was revised, with a chrome bumper and a chrome-trim front grille becoming standard equipment. In an engineering change, the three-quarter and one-ton trucks were switched from 16.5inch to 16inch wheels in order to be suited to a wider range of commercially available tyres. The Cheyenne trim level was discontinued but Custom Deluxe, Scottsdale and Silverado (pictured) were still offered

MIDDLE, ABOVE AND RIGHT: The CUCV represented General Motors' first major light-truck military vehicle production since World War II. They were assembled from existing heavy duty light commercial truck parts and came in four basic body styles: pickup, utility, ambulance body and chassis cab. The M1009 model (pictured) was a Chevrolet K5 Blazer uprated to three-quarter-ton capacity. GM produced around 70,000 CUCVs from 1983 to 1986 for model years 1984–1987 though most were model year 1984. Chevrolet continued to build CUCVs in low numbers from 1986 to 1996

ABOVE AND BELOW: Of the CUCV pickups the M1008 was the basic cargo truck. With the exception of the M1009, the trucks were all rated as 1.25ton even though some of them had payloads in excess of that. The M1008 was the most numerous of the CUCV truck types and was often fitted with troop seats for eight in the bed. Military fitments included a brush bar, front and rear tow hooks, and a pintle hitch. All CUCV trucks were powered by GM's 6.2L J-series Detroit Diesel V8 engine

ABOVE: American Motors made the CJ-10 pickup from 1981-1986 with a choice of three engines; 151ci four-cylinder, 258ci six-cylinder and a 3.3l in-line six diesel built by Nissan. The CJ-10 started its production in South Bend, Indiana, before being moved south to Mexico in 1983 where this 1984 model was assembled

The midsize Dodge Dakota appeared in 1987. It came with a 96 hp 2.2L I-4 or a 3.9L 90-degree V6, which was essentially a 5.2 V8 with a couple of cylinders missing (it marked the end of Slant Six in D/W-series too). Two years later, the Dakota convertible arrived for a two-year run, and the club cab and rear-drive only pickup collaboration with Shelby (with a 175hp 318) followed. By 1992 the 318 was now a 230 hp 5.2L Magnum

ABOVE: The Chevrolet S-10 is a compact pickup that was the first US-built compact pickup from the big three American automakers. It was first introduced as a quarter-ton pickup in 1981 for the 1982 model year

ABOVE: The GMC version of the Chevrolet S-10 was the S-15 that was later renamed the GMC Sonoma. A high-performance version would be released in 1991 and given the name of GMC Syclone

ABOVE: The 1989 GMC S15 Sierra Classic, with the optional sports appearance package from around the time, GMC introduced both the GMC S15 and Chevrolet S10 to compete in this compact pickup truck segment of the market. It was intended to offer excellent payloads, fuel efficiency and performance on a budget in a compact vehicle

ABOVE: The 1989 GMC Sierra C/K 1500 is the smallest of the Sierras and available with either a 78 or 84in bed. It is powered by a V6 or diesel V8 engine. The C/K 1500 comes in two cab types; regular and extended. The Sierra C/K 2500 is designed for medium-duty use and provides a greater payload and towing capacity than the 1500 series. The Sierra C/K 2500 is also available in regular and extended cab versions. For heavy-duty use, there is the 1989 GMC Sierra C/K 3500. Offering the largest payload and towing capacities in the 1989 Sierra line-up, power is supplied by one of two V8 engines

RIGHT: The 1989 GMC R/V Bonus Cab duallie was one of the third-generation C/K series marketed by Chevrolet and GMC divisions, primarily as pickup trucks in half-ton, three-quarter-ton, and one-ton payload series. These C/K pickup trucks were offered in two cab designs, three bed configurations and three wheelbase lengths. For 1989, all R/V pickup trucks (pictured) underwent their most visible facelift since 1981. While retaining the same fenders and hood from 1981 to 1988, the grille was redesigned to give a nearly flush appearance, with much of the trim painted black. In another nomenclature change, the R/V series would adopt the 2500/3500 series payload series for both GMC and Chevrolet